THE BOOK OF THE TOAD

The Book of the Toad

A Natural and Magical History of Toad-Human Relations

ROBERT M. DEGRAAFF

Park Street Press

ROCHESTER·VERMONT

Park Street Press
One Park Street
Rochester, Vermont 05767

Library of Congress Cataloging-in-Publication Data
DeGraaff, Robert M.
    The book of the toad / Robert M. DeGraaff
      p. cm.
    Includes bibliographical references (p.   ) and index.
    ISBN 0-89281-261-3 (cloth) : $19.95
    1. Toads. 2. Toads—Folklore 3. Toads—Literary collections.
    4. Bufonidae. 5. Bufonidae—Folklore 6. Bufonidae—Literary
collections.   I. Title.
    QL668.E227D44 1991
    597.8'7—dc20
                                             91–18064
                                                CIP

Printed and bound in Hong Kong

10 9 8 7 6 5 4 3 2 1

Park Street Press is a division of Inner Traditions International, Ltd.

Distributed to the book trade in the United States by American International Distribution Corporation (AIDC)

Distributed to the book trade in Canada by Book Center, Inc., Montreal, Quebec

Text Design by Virginia L. Scott

Art on pages ii and iii: *Leaping Toads* illustration by Judy Jensen, 1990.
Art on page 5: *Natterjack,* from *The Century Dictionary and Cyclopedia* (twelve vols.), 1889–1913; reproduced from Harold H. Hart, *Animal Art in the Public Domain,* copyright 1983 by Hart Publishing Company, New York. Photo by Judith DeGraaff.
Art on page 69: Illustration from *Hortus Sanitatis,* 1491; Chapin Library, Williams College.

Acknowledgment is made for permission to quote, or to quote from, the following works:
(NOTE: this list includes all literary permissions, and courtesy acknowledgments, in the order that the literature appears in the text.)

Richard Wilbur: "The Death of a Toad," from *Ceremony and Other Poems,* copyright 1950 and renewed 1978 by Richard Wilbur, reprinted by permission of Harcourt Brace Jovanovich, Inc.
Joseph Wood Krutch: passage from *The Desert Year,* copyright 1951 by William Sloane Associates; reprinted by permission of William Morrow & Co., Inc.
Scott Bates: "The Perfect Toad," copyright 1951 by Scott Bates; first published in Furioso, Winter 1951.
Susan Fromberg Schaeffer: "Narcissus Toad," "Earring Toad," and "The Little Child's Toad," reprinted with permission of Macmillan Publishing Company from *The Rhymes and Runes of the Toad,* by Susan Fromberg Schaeffer. Text copyright 1975 by Susan Fromberg Schaeffer.
Kenneth Grahame: "The Song of Mr. Toad," from *The Wind in the Willows;* first published in 1908 by Methuen Books, London.
A.C. Benson: passage from "The Toad," from *The Poems of A.C. Benson,* published in 1909 by John Lane.

T.J.C. Beebee: passages from *The Natterjack Toad*, published in 1983 by Oxford University Press.

Donald Finkel: "Spring Song," reprinted with permission of Atheneum Publishers, an imprint of Macmillan Publishing Company, from *A Joyful Noise*, by Donald Finkel. Copyright 1965, 1966 by Donald Finkel. Originally published in *The New Yorker*.

Arthur N. Bragg: material from *Gnomes of the Night: the Spadefoot Toads*, published in 1965 by the University of Pennsylvania Press.

Jane Taylor: passage from "The Toad's Journal," from *The Library of Poetry and Song*, III, published in 1925 by Doubleday, Page.

Dante Gabriel Rossetti: passage from "Jenny," from *The Collected Works of Dante Gabriel Rossetti*, I, published in 1886 by Ellis and Scrutton.

Arthur Koestler: material from *The Case of the Midwife Toad*, published by Random House, Inc., copyright 1971 by Arthur Koestler.

William Butler Yeats: passage from "Sailing to Byzantium," reprinted with permission of Macmillan Publishing Company from *The Poems of W.B. Yeats: A New Edition*, edited by Richard J. Finneran, 1989.

John Burroughs: passage from "The Song of the Toad," from *Bird and Bough*, published by Houghton Mifflin Company, copyright 1906 by John Burroughs.

Philip Raisor: "Toads Breeding, Thumb Swelling," originally published in Poetry Northwest, 1982; reprinted with permission of the editor of *Poetry Northwest*, and of Philip Raisor.

George Orwell: excerpt from "Some Thoughts on the Common Toad" in *Shooting an Elephant and Other Essays* by George Orwell, copyright 1946 by Sonia Brownell Orwell and renewed 1974 by Sonia Orwell, reprinted by permission of Harcourt Brace Jovanovich, Inc., Martin Secker & Warburg Ltd., and the estate of the late Sonia Brownell Orwell.

Charles Martin: "Orgy with Toads," originally published in *Poetry* and copyrighted in 1973 by The Modern Poetry Association; reprinted with permission of the editor of *Poetry*, and of Charles Martin.

Thornton Burgess: "The Little Toads Start Out To See the World," and "Old Mr. Toad's Mistake," from *The Adventures of Old Mr. Toad*, copyright Thornton W. Burgess, 1916, 1944; published by Grosset & Dunlap, 1916.

Taylor Alexander: passage from "Observations on the Feeding Behavior of Bufo marinus (Linne)," 1964, reprinted with permission of the editor of *Herpetologica*.

A.A. Milne: passage from *Toad of Toad Hall*, reprinted with permission of Charles Scribner's Sons, an imprint of Macmillan Publishing Company. Copyright 1929 Charles Scribner's Sons: copyright renewed © 1957 Dorothy Daphine Milne. British rights by permission of Curtis Brown, Ltd., London; copyright ©1929 by A.A. Milne.

Edmund Spenser: passages from *The Faerie Queene*, from *The Poetical Works of Edmund Spenser*, edited by J.C. Smith, and published by the Clarendon Press, Oxford, 1909.

Ambrose Bierce: passage from *The Devil's Dictionary*, from *The Collected Writings of Ambrose Bierce*, edited by C. Fadiman, and published by the Citadel Press, 1946.

R. Howard Hunt: passage from "Toad Sanctuary in a Tarantula Burrow," 1980, reprinted with permission from *Natural History*, Vol. 89, No. 3; copyright the American Museum of Natural History, 1980.

Elizabeth Bishop: "Giant Toad," from *The Complete Poems*, 1927-1979, copyright 1983, reprinted with permission of Farrar, Straus and Giroux, Inc.

Oliver Goldsmith: passage from *Life of Nash*, from *The Works of Oliver Goldsmith*, edited by P. Cunningham, and published by Harper & Brothers, New York, 1900.

Felix Mann: passage from "The Homoeopathic Toad," 1959, reprinted with permission of the editor of *The British Homoeopathic Journal*.

Lynn Thorndike: passages from *A History of Magic and Experimental Science*, I-VIII, 1923-1958, reprinted with permission of Columbia University Press.

Conrad Hilberry: "Toads," originally published in *The Kenyon Review*, 1982; reprinted with permission of Conrad Hilberry.

X.J. Kennedy: "A Visit to the Gingerbread House," from *The Phantom Ice Cream Man*, 1979; copyright X.J. Kennedy, 1975, 1977, 1978, 1979, and reprinted with permission of Curtis Brown, Ltd.

J. Stern (ed.): paraphrase of "The Three Feathers," from *The Complete Grimm's Fairy Tales*, 1944,

The Book of the Toad is dedicated
to the poet, Richard Wilbur,
whose poem, "The Death of a Toad,"
gave birth to this work.

CONTENTS

ACKNOWLEDGMENTS

My deepest thanks to herpetologists, zookeepers, art museum staff persons, artists, and poets around the world who aided me in my great toad hunt with courtesy and enthusiasm, supplying materials and information;

to faculty colleagues and friends Nils Ekfelt, Lynn Ekfelt, George Frear, Aden Hayes, Helen Hirsch, Edward Pierce, and others who helped me with translations and with photographs;

to St. Lawrence University, and deans George Gibson, Thomas Coburn, and G. Andrew Rembert, for university resources and services put at my disposal;

to the Owen D. Young reference librarians and interlibrary loan people;

to Gail Colvin and Laurie Olmstead, by all odds the two best word processors the world has yet seen;

to Samuel B. Shapiro and Mary Shapiro, who proofread the manuscript;

and finally, to my family, who suffered me throughout the long toad ordeal.

Robert M. DeGraaff
September 1991

THE TOAD
Pablo Picasso
lithograph, 1949
Collection of Morton G.Neumann
Photo by Michael Tropea

PREFACE

Two years ago, while cutting the grass in my backyard with a power mower, I happened to run over a toad. By the time my fingers found the switch, the blades of the mower had slashed the animal badly. I do not regard myself as a sentimental person, but I was troubled as I bent down to examine it. It wasn't just that I had unwittingly killed an ally against the hordes of mosquitoes, gnats, and flies that plague our summers. It was mostly the rush of blood that affected me, making it dramatically clear that what at first glance looked to be a clod of earth was actually a living being, unlike the cold, formaldahyde-filled frogs we had dissected in high school biology class.

There in the backyard, I picked the toad up carefully and carried him to the shade of a nearby lilac bush. He was still alive, but did not move. No doubt by this time he was incapable of moving, yet it seemed to me rather that he *chose* not to move; indeed, he seemed to have a real dignity. When I had finished the mowing and returned to the lilac bush, I found the toad—as I had expected—dead, just in the spot where I had set him down.

It was one of those odd coincidences—or perhaps what Jungians would call one of those synchronistic events—that within a few weeks of the incident with the mower I came across a poem by Richard Wilbur describing an experience very similar to mine.

The Death of a Toad

A toad the power mower caught,
Chewed and clipped of a leg, with a hobbling hop has got
To the garden verge, and sanctuaried him,
Under the cineraria leaves, in the shade
Of the ashen heartshaped leaves, in a dim,
Low, and a final glade.

The rare original heartsblood goes,
Spends on the earthen hide, in the folds and wizenings, flows
In the gutters of the banked and staring eyes. He lies
As still as if he would return to stone,
And soundlessly attending, dies
Toward some deep monotone,

Toward misted and ebullient seas
And cooling shores, toward lost Amphibia's emperies.
Day dwindles, drowning, and at length is gone
In the wide and antique eyes, which still appear
To watch, across the castrate lawn
The haggard daylight steer.

Richard Wilbur

The poem expresses very well both the sense of the toad's dignity that had so impressed me, and its essential earthiness. But what most delighted me was the poet's image of a lush prehistoric green world over which the toad presides; our neat suburban lawns appear as a diminished and tame setting for this visiting monarch from an earlier, grander, more vital world.

In that moment Wilbur's poem turned me into a confirmed bufophile, and in the months of teaching college literature courses that followed, I seemed to find references to toads everywhere. Eventually I decided to put together an article on literary treatments of the toad. Before long, however, the project seemed too limited in scope, and I

BUFO AMERICANUS COPEI
Terence Shortt
watercolor on paper
12.7 x 17.8 cm., 1942
Collection of Martina R. Norelli
Photo by Gene Young

resolved instead to write a history of toad-human relations. In the process, it proved impossible to avoid compiling a brief scientific survey of the toad as well. If the resulting compendium of toad lore and literature serves to advance *Bufo's* standing and to impart something of the awe, keen interest, and delight that have sustained this study, it will have served its purpose well.

INTRODUCTION

*I cannot tell by what logic we call a toad, a bear, or an elephant ugly;
they being created in those outward shapes and figures which best
express the actions of their inward frames; and having passed that
general visitation of God, who saw that all that He had made was
good.*

SIR THOMAS BROWNE, 1642

It is a fact that the toad has been a much abused animal,
particularly in western civilization. By the time of Shakespeare, its
ugliness was already proverbial, an automatic metaphor for anything
loathsome. Nor was its image improved by its reputation for being
highly poisonous. It took no great leap for the sixteenth- and seventeenth-century imagination to conclude that a creature so repulsive and
venomous must, consequently, be evil. In some contexts, the toad was
even regarded as an embodiment of Satan himself: a woman with a pet
toad in seventeenth-century England would most likely have been
accused of being a witch, the toad her demon-familiar. Milton's
Paradise Lost describes Satan as "Squat like a Toad, close at the ear of
Eve," breathing his poisonous vapors in an attempt to infect her fancy
and prepare her for the Fall.

Such attitudes were, at least in part, a result of ignorance; but even
had there been a greater open-mindedness and scientific curiosity, it is

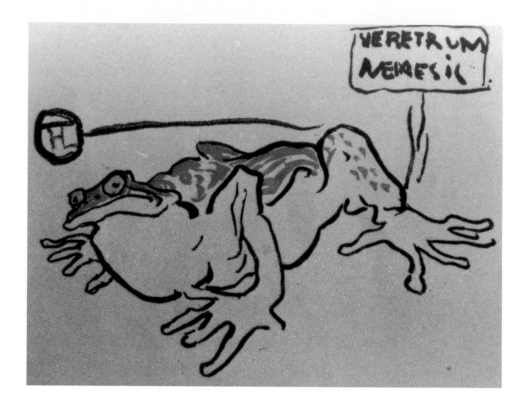

doubtful that very much would have been learned about the toad. As Joseph Wood Krutch has written,

> the most important reason why there are so many gaps in the available life histories of even the commoner animals is less the perversity of professors than the fact that there are an awful lot of these common creatures and that actually to follow their lives from day to day is a very difficult, time-consuming task.
>
> [*The Desert Year:* 109]

Of all the common creatures, the toad is one of the most elusive. It is generally nocturnal—seldom seen in daylight, when it hides itself underground or in some burrow. Furthermore, except in very warm climates, it hibernates during the winter months. Thus for much of the day and an extended part of the year it is simply not visible to the average person. For the most part, then, human contacts with toads throughout

ILLUSTRATION FOR "LES DEUX SOEURS LEGENDAIRES'
Le Figaro Illustré
Henri de Toulouse-Lautrec
Mai, 1896
Courtesy Case Western Reserve University Library
Photo by Carl Mariani

history have been peripheral—on the fringes, not at the heart, of human affairs. Yet when one investigates these contacts, as they are reflected in art, literature, and folklore, one finds a wealth of fascinating material.

Not that the toad has always been maligned. There is a good deal of evidence that in early Asiatic cultures and in the pre-Columbian civilizations of the Americas the toad was regarded as a divinity, the great primeval Earth Mother, the source and the end of all life. Even in the Christian era, the toad has had its human allies and sometimes taken on positive symbolic values. Some have seen in its ability to metamorphose an emblem of Christ's resurrection. Others (Henri Toulouse-Lautrec for one) have found beauty in its very ugliness.

Still, despite the presence of a minority of sympathizers, the prevailing Western view of toads, whether as foul and loathsome creatures in themselves or as emblems of the demonic, has been decidedly negative. Not until the late Victorian period, and more fully in the twentieth century, was there a major shift in human sensibility, one that allows us to accept the toad for what it is and respect it as a legitimate member of the natural world to which we all belong. Only in our age is the protection of certain toads as "endangered species" even thinkable.

The first section of this book is chiefly meant to familiarize readers with the actual toad animal. It is by no means intended as a complete scientific analysis, but as a basis for the second section—a more or less chronological survey of interactions between toads and the human race.

PART I:
A NATURAL HISTORY

TOAD OR FROG?

In one moment I've seen what has hitherto been
Enveloped in absolute mystery,
And without extra charge I will give you at large
A lesson in Natural History.

Lewis Carroll, "The Hunting of the Snark"

So far as I can tell, there is no foolproof way to differentiate toads and frogs from either a scientific or from a nontechnical point of view. The formal taxonomy of the class Amphibia is extremely complex and subject to continuing debate and disagreement. Besides the Salientia (or Anura), the order of tailless amphibians to which frogs and toads belong, the class includes the Gymnophiona, wormlike burrowers without limbs, and the Caudata, tailed amphibians with limbs (such as newts and salamanders). Here is *Bufo*'s bio-tree:

Phylum Chordata
    Subphylum Vertebrata
      Class Amphibia
        Superorder Lissamphibia
          Order Salientia (Anura)
            Suborder Acosmanura
              Family Ranidae ("true frogs")
              Family Bufonidae ("true toads")

Although all anurans have the same general shape, they exhibit a wide range of variation not only in physical characteristics such as size, color, skull and bone structure, type of tongue (if any), shape of pupil, and so forth, but also in features of their lifestyle, such as habitat and breeding behavior. Classification is, therefore, intricate and complicated. The standard *Introduction to Herpetology,* by Goin, Goin, and Zug, lists four suborders of anurans, made up of twenty-three families, with some families containing as many as seven subfamilies—the whole comprising approximately 2,510 separate species. Although scientists generally use the term "frog" for any anuran, it is in fact the single family known as the *Ranidae,* whose members are usually referred to as the "true frogs,"while members of the family *Bufonidae* are often called "true toads." Actually, of course, the term "true" here is meaningless. Many species outside the *Ranidae* are commonly called "frogs" and many nonbufonids "toads." There is no apparent logic in the idea that somehow these two families have the only legitimate claim to these titles, as though, for example, the American toad (of the *Bufonidae*) were the real thing and the Eastern spadefoot toad (of the *Pelobatidae*) a counterfeit.

Whatever the ambiguities of systematics, common parlance seems confident in its ability to distinguish frogs and toads. Of the several foreign-language dictionaries I consulted, all made the same distinction: The frog is essentially a water creature, with a moist, smooth skin and long, powerful hind legs for leaping; the toad, except for its tadpole stage and breeding periods, is primarily terrestrial. Its skin is drier and rougher than that of a frog, and its hind legs are shorter and weaker, so that it can only hop. No country kid would hesitate to call a toad a toad (though, of course, such a system of classification is too oversimplified to be scientifically valid).

In selecting materials for these pages, I have tried to be just as decisive as a country kid. This was usually easy in the case of literature: whatever creature the writer might have been looking at or thinking of, in a poem a toad is a toad is a toad. It was often much more difficult in the case of art, where the animal represented —whatever its name— might or might not be a toad. Particularly complicated were the ancient representations, whose "titles" have usually been provided by modern museum curators or art connoisseurs without extensive backgrounds in herpetology. Here I occasionally trusted my own instincts and included a work I believed to represent a toad, regardless of its museum title. In a few other instances I have included images of anurans that are not clearly identifiable as either frogs or toads, but that I believed to have some symbolic meaning as amphibians —a meaning in which the toad would share. In recounting factual material, I have concentrated on the *Bufonidae* but have not hesitated to include a few other species that both look like toads and are commonly referred to as toads. (I did cheat a little in including the Surinam toad, *Pipa pipa*, which I found irresistible because of its wonderfully bizarre breeding behavior, despite the fact that it lives only in water.) I have excluded "tree-toads," which are now usually referred to by scientists as "tree-frogs," nor have I used the Texas "horned toad," which is in reality a lizard.

The Perfect Toad

The sun caught the pond
In a second of sky
With its boreas down
And its cumuli dry

Fast asleep
On the edge of the pond
A Toad felt the touch
Of a second of sun

He opened his eyes
And raised his head
At this precise moment
I'm perfect he said

He closed his eyes
And destroyed the view
I'm perfect he thought
At this moment too

                    Scott Bates

"European Common Toad,
European Green Toad, and
Natterjack Toad"
from Animals
edited by Jim Harter
Copyright 1979 by Dover
Publications, Inc., New York
Photo by Judith DeGraaff

As is perhaps obvious, I find the common toad a far more interesting animal than the common frog. For one thing, it lives for the most part on land; it is my neighbor. And then it is so much more sensible. None of this froglike squawking and diving into the water to hide in mud and leaves at the bottom of a pond. You can confront a toad; you can have a tête-à-tête with him. And indeed human beings have established relationships with toads, communing each evening with some resident toad under the back porch and perhaps feeding him a few choice insects. Except in terms of their menu, toads are no fly-by-nighters, but decent creatures of steady habits who make regular rounds to established burrows and feeding places; they can be counted on. Pet toads have lived as long as thirty-five years, witnessing the passage of generations of dogs and cats.

Toads are steady. A. F. Bennett found that when a frog (*Rana pipiens*) and a toad (*Bufo boreas*) were released simultaneously in a classroom, the frog leapt wildly about, covering three times the distance of the toad in the first thirty seconds. But after two minutes the frog showed signs of wearing out, and by the end of five minutes it was totally exhausted. The toad, on the other hand, maintained a slow and steady pace that it could continue indefinitely. The hare-frog is a sprinter, its metabolism anaerobic, the tortoise-toad a jogger, allied in its aerobic endurance to birds, mammals, and "higher" forms of life. The toad's heart is bigger than that of the frog, its cardiovascular system more developed [Bennett: 453].

Narcissus Toad

There was a time when toad
Was only 2,000 years old
And the world was only 2,000 years old,
And there were not even

Trees, or grass, or animals,
Only ashy, grassy fields,
And blank, mirrory ponds.
Whenever toad passed one of these ponds

He would plunk himself down
And call out, "Earth,
Let us celebrate a birthday,
For though you are large, and round,

I am beautiful, and a wonder,
And can walk where I please."
Then the winds would rustle
As if giving assent

And toad agreed with himself
That these days were good.
Gradually, the earth became greener
And columns stood on it

And things moved in the shadows
But toad barely noticed
Because he was busy taking note of himself
Who could go where he pleased.

One day, he looked into a pond, and there
Was something just like him,
But bigger, and made out of jade.
"And who are you, and what do you think!"

Demanded toad in rage.
"I am frog," the creature answered,
"And bigger than you, and may swim,
And may go where I please."

Toad felt totally wounded.
He called up his old friends,
The winds, and they called up the tides,
Frog called up his new friends,

The clouds, and soon the new leaves
Of the trees were rustling and rustling.
"Stop this," said the World,
"Or there will be a terrible storm."

But they would not stop
And puffed up their cheeks
Like storm clouds, and the storm tides
Swelled and swelled and covered the earth.

On the third day, frog,
Feeling triumphant,
Took time off from his frog kick
To wave with a leg

To an ark sailing placidly by,
But the two little toads,
Hidden in the hold
Between the sacks full of barley

Kept perfectly still.

Susan Fromberg Schaeffer

In some ways, toads are smarter than frogs. They have to be: they are slower and much more vulnerable.

> Compared with his nearest rival, the frog, the toad reacts more promptly and learns more readily. Toads can figure out a maze far more quickly than frogs can. They discover after eight or nine trials that a glass barrier cannot be passed, whereas frogs keep bumping their noses against it. When set on a high table, toads will peer cautiously over the edge, appearing to estimate the drop, and then refuse to jump. Frogs will fling themselves off anything. . . . another indication of the toad's mental capacities is that he is easily tamed. Toads in captivity learn to come out of hiding when called and to feed from the hand. They also seem to enjoy being petted and stroked.
>
> [Colby: 65]

When Edward Greding tested three species of *Rana* against three species of *Bufo* in his laboratory, he found that all three species of *Bufo* were able to acquire information more rapidly and retain it longer. Greding's results also suggested, though he was unable to reach definitive conclusions here, that there might be individual differences in the rate of learning [Greding: 208]. In other words, just as common sense would lead one to expect, some toads are smarter than others.

The Song of Mr. Toad

The world has held great Heroes,
  As history-books have showed;
But never a name to go down to fame
  Compared with that of Toad!

The clever men at Oxford
  Know all that there is to be knowed.
But they none of them know one half as much
  As intelligent Mr. Toad!

The animals sat in the Ark and cried,
  Their tears in torrents flowed.
Who was it said, "There's land ahead?"
  Encouraging Mr. Toad!

The Army all saluted
  As they marched along the road.
Was it the King? Or Kitchener?
  No, It was Mr. Toad!

The Queen and her Ladies-in-waiting
  Sat at the window and sewed.
She cried, "Look! who's that handsome man?"
  They answered, "Mr. Toad."

Kenneth Grahame

TOAD EVOLUTION

Thou seem'st the heir of centuries, hatched out
With aeons on thy track;
The dust of ages compasses about
Thy lean and shrivelled back.

            A. C. Benson, "The Toad"

If the scientists are right, we owe the toad a great debt: his forebears, as the first vertebrates to leave the water some three hundred million or more years ago, led us all up onto dry land. Without them, who knows where we would be now? Since the Devonian period, however, the toad has not always been treated with the honor due a pioneer. With many enemies and minimal defenses, he has survived by adapting to fill almost any available biological niche. This is no doubt why, even though many anuran species have become extinct, there are still over twenty-five hundred surviving variations on the basic toad-frog animal. Some of them live entirely in or near water; some live in trees; some live on land, while others spend most of their time underground. They populate forests, mountains, and even deserts. Geographically, there are indigenous toad populations on every major land mass on the planet except Australia and Antarctica. Although about 80 percent of anuran species live in the teeming tropics, where the amphibians probably arose, anurans can be found within the Arctic Circle right up to the permafrost line [Porter: 245]. In 1975, as

photographer Juan Muñoz approached Smuggler's Lake, about thirty miles north of Ketchikan, Alaska, he was startled to find several small ponds inhabited by many thousands of breeding Western toads *(Bufo boreas)*.

The Yosemite toad *(Bufo canorus)* may be found in California's Sierra Nevada at elevations of over eleven thousand feet, commonly walking over snowdrifts to get to its breeding pools [Sherman and Morton: 73]. Toads in the Andes and Himalayas may be found at even higher elevations.

A survival adaptation used by many anuran species is protective coloration; toads of North America, especially, exhibit a mottled

TOAD HUGGING A BALL
Alan Barrett-Danes
Photo by Alan Barrett-Danes

TOAD ORGY
1975
Photo by Juan Muñoz

texture and drab shades of brown, gray, and rust that help them blend in with their environment and thus escape detection. Often a range of color variation can be found within a single species, and some species have the ability to alter their skin shade to suit changing conditions.

The tailless amphibians of the tropics, however, are often distinguished by their flaming colors, ranging from bright blues and purples to yellows, oranges, and reds, with various flashy color combinations. There is often a correlation between the brightness of the colors and the potency of the venom in these species—the colors, in this case, serving as a warning to would-be predators. But though the tropical toads and frogs may be more colorful, our local toads are by no means visually dull.

The Natterjack Toad

The ways in which a particular species has adapted to particular conditions may be seen in the case of the sun-loving natterjack toad *(Bufo calamita)*, a species to which an entire volume has been devoted (Beebee, 1983). This toad prefers a hot and dry climate, but its unique adaptations have enabled it to inhabit some sixteen countries of western Europe, from Spain north to Sweden and Scotland. It gravitates to open terrain with loose soil, such as the heaths and dunes of England. Here the lack of vegetation allows it to soak up more sun, either directly, for which it has become partly diurnal, or indirectly, from the sun-baked sand. Both tadpoles and adults can withstand higher temperatures than those tolerated by other European toad species, and Beebee reports seeing adults regulate their body temperature by moving in or out of the mouths of their burrows to absorb just the right dosage of rays.

The loose soil natterjacks prefer is not only a heat source, but also an escape from the cold, as they have developed a double set of tubercles on the back of their hind-leg ankles that serve as digging tools. They are capable of slowly disappearing into the ground by throwing up dirt with their hind feet, or of pulling soil out of a hole with their front feet—whichever way the spirit moves them. In England, they have been dug out of hibernation from depths of one to two feet, while in Germany, where the winters are more severe, they have been found as much as ten feet under.

Perhaps partly because the specialized habitat suitable to them is relatively rare in Europe, these toads are less solitary than many other species, typically living in colonies. A single burrow may accommodate several or even several dozen individuals. Young juveniles like to pile up in mounds to take their summer sunbaths and while such behavior may have survival value in helping them to get warm without drying out, it does seem an amiable habit. Even in its mating behavior, the natterjack demonstrates a certain refinement. While in other species jealous males may try to unhorse a mounted male, and females may even drown under a regular mountain of ardent males, an amplexed natterjack couple may swim in peace past any number of lusty bachelors without being disturbed.

Other distinctive features of the natterjack are its unique eye color—gold-green, rather than the prevailing gold-orange—and the yellow stripe that runs down its back—not, in this case, indicating cowardice. These traits may or may not have any survival value, but the characteristic smell of the natterjack's skin secretions, which Beebee describes as similar to gunpowder or burnt india rubber, may be useful in discouraging some predators. This toad's most distinctive feature, however, must surely be its very short hind legs with their unusually high number of blood vessels, which allow it to run rather than hop— a gait far more suitable in loose soil for toad-the-hunter.

> The sight of prey . . . excites natterjacks in a way that little else can do. The toad immediately assumes an alert rigid posture with head craned in the direction of the potential meal. Toes on the hind feet often twitch quite violently as the seconds pass . . .   [Beebee: 63]

It is unfortunate that despite its specialization in habitats that would not seem valuable to us, the natterjack is under fire both from human civilization and from nature herself. Although Great Britain declared it an endangered species in 1975, and anyone wishing to tamper with toads or tadpoles now needs a special license, there is no effective machinery in place to protect the natterjack's shrinking habitat. Housing developments and golf courses continue to proliferate, bringing with them increased traffic, pesticides, and drainage systems that destroy breeding ponds. The gradual return of open heath to forest, with or without human aid, renders an increasing area unsuitable for natterjacks. The shadier country attracts the common European toad *(Bufo bufo),* which breeds earlier in the spring, producing tadpoles who greedily devour hatching natterjack spawn. As similar trends are also occurring in much of Europe, it may be that *Bufo calamita* will eventually be forced, like the Apaches, to retreat to semideserts (such as those of Andalusia) as a last stronghold.

Spadefoot Toads

Spring Song

For a toad enjoys a finer prospect than another creature to

compensate his lack . . . For there are stones, whose constitu-
ent particles are toads.

Christopher Smart

B'york! but it's lovely under the leaf—
cool, green, slimy, sleeping,
quietly breathing at all my pores—
a jade toad in a rainy garden.

Down here, ceiling zero,
pulse steady, breathing slow,
heart smiling under his harness,
brain grinning behind the bone,

down here, in the dead of winter,
nothing happens, honey of time
slowly, sweetly melts and oozes
in the vein.

Tall in the saddle, hulking stranger,
looking for trouble, blind with anger,
you who think to stand between
the sun and me: think again.

Ten feet up you cannot see
further than your bleeding fist;
blows leap out from every tree,
the night is your antagonist.

Sad Goliath, gloomy champion,
lost in an unfriendly wood,
riding high, riding handsome,
ten feet up from where my gleaming
stones can do you any good,

far away your love is sleeping,
far away your king is dead,
your eye is almost shut with weeping,
your foot is bruised against my head.

Donald Finkel

Zapato y sapos
[Shoe and Toads]
Francisco Toledo
acrylic on paper on masonite
55.8 x 75.5 cm., 1972
Archer M. Huntington Art Gallery
The University of Texas at Austin
Gift of Barbara Duncan, 1977
Photo by George Holmes

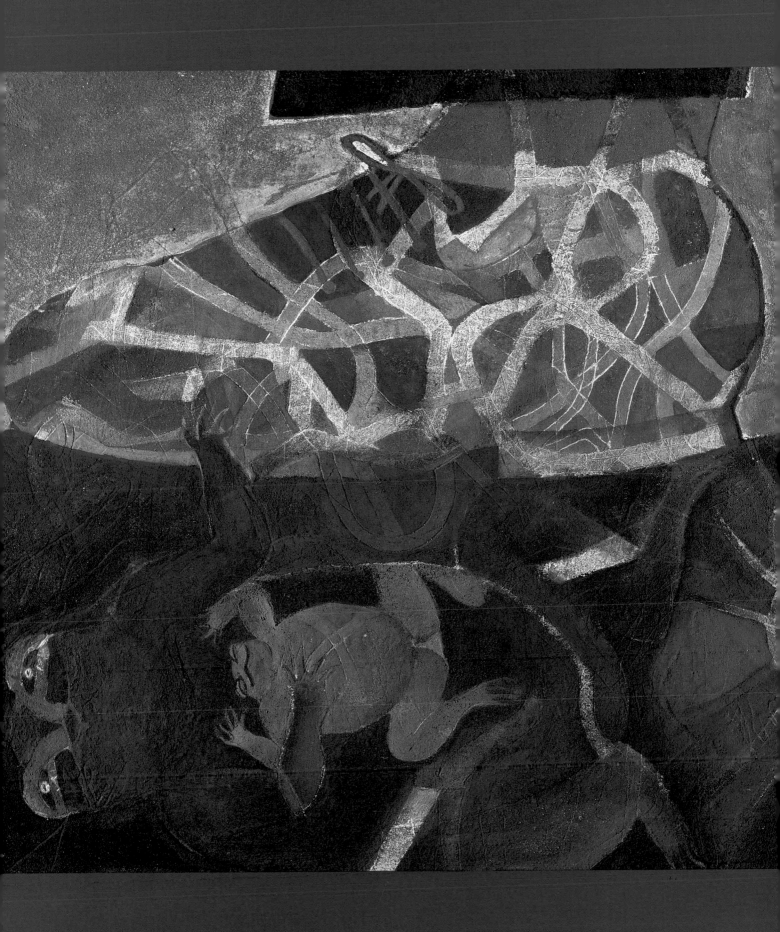

A group of toads with a strong claim on the title of most well-adjusted are the spadefoots of the United States (genus *Scaphiopus*), with some seven or eight local species, located chiefly in the grasslands of the central plains and the desert or semidesert areas of the Southwest (there is also one species of "Eastern spadefoot"). Though they are not bufonids but members of the more primitive family Pelobatidae, no one has ever tried to call them frogs (even if one writer does facetiously suggest that they might be called "froads" or "trogs"). While it is true that most of them have certain froggy features, such as smooth, moist skins and heavily webbed hind feet, they are probably the most land-based of all the anurans—indeed, spending most of their time not so much *on* land as *under* it. The webs are there to aid in moving not water but sandy soil. At any rate, the numerous scientists and science popularizers whose imaginations have been stirred to write about these little creatures always call them toads. Some writers, indeed, have been inspired to more creative sobriquets: certainly the most sprightly of these is Arthur N. Bragg's title for his delightful book about the spadefoots, *Gnomes of the Night* (1965).

The spadefoots, unlike any other toads, have pupils that close vertically, like those of a cat; their night vision is extraordinary. They also have, but in an exaggerated form, something several other species of toads also have—a horny growth on the hind feet that is helpful in digging. In *Scaphiopus* this resembles a small shovel or spade, whence their common name. In some species the appendage is about as long as it is wide; in others it is much longer, but more narrow.

With their built-in equipment, spadefoots are able to dig themselves under in a remarkably short time—if the soil is loose and sandy, a matter of seconds. Their method is not fastidious, but very effective: they scrape the dirt out from under themselves and toss it over their own heads, gradually displacing themselves into the ground.

Since the greatest threat to toad life in desert areas is death by dehydration, the spadefoot's ability to dig is obviously valuable. During long periods of drought, spadefoots may delve as far down as twelve feet to reach the soil moisture they need. This they soak up, in typical anuran fashion, through a special patch of skin below the belly area (no toads can "drink," in our sense of the term). In addition, they have developed an amazing tolerance for their own urea and in a pinch may reabsorb moisture from their own urine, which they retain in a special holding tank. With all these advantages, as well as the ability to breathe through their skins, the spadefoots can do very nicely underground for extended periods of time. Since they hibernate for the winter months and aestivate when it gets too dry, they may be there as long as ten or eleven months of the year, defying cold, heat, and drought.

(It is said that Belzoni, the traveller in Egypt, discovered a living toad in a temple, which had been for ages buried in the sand.)

In a land for antiquities greatly renowned
A traveller had dug wide and deep under ground,
A temple, for ages entombed, to disclose,—
When, lo! he disturbed, in its secret repose,
A toad, from whose journal it plainly appears
It had lodged in that mansion some thousands of years.

Jane Taylor, "The Toad's Journal"

Of course there are many stories of toads discovered under building foundations, apparently immured in rock and yet able to survive for decades or even centuries. In the course of time such tales easily become mythic or take on symbolic meaning. For the speaker in Dante Gabriel Rossetti's "Jenny," for example, soliloquizing over a sleeping prostitute, the toad-in-stone suggests the ugly reality of male lust:

Yet, Jenny, looking long at you,
The woman almost fades from view.
A cipher of man's changeless sum
Of lust, past, present, and to come,
Is left. A riddle that one shrinks
To challenge from the scornful sphinx.

Like a toad within a stone
Seated while time crumbles on;
Which sits there since the earth was curs'd
For Man's trangression at the first;
Which, living through all centuries,
Not once has seen the sun arise;

Whose life, to its cold circle charmed,
The earth's whole summers have not warmed;
Which always—whitherso the stone
Be flung—sits there, deaf, blind, alone;—
Aye, and shall not be driven out
Till that which shuts him round about
Break at the very Master's stroke,
And the dust thereof vanish as smoke,
And the seed of Man vanish as dust:—
Even so within this world is Lust.

Yet even within this context of conservative Christian morality, the toad suggests something seminal, of the earth, earthy—a symbolic value that at other times and in other places has been accepted and approved rather than condemned. But of this more anon.

In real life, two eighteenth-century experimenters, suffering from a bad case of scientific curiosity, did eventually bury some toads in plaster and limestone to see just how long they could survive. The answer was one year, more or less. No animal, obviously, can go without food indefinitely, and toads are not able to eat while underground. So, like the ghost of Hamlet's father, the spadefoots are "doomed for a certain term to walk the night."

Of course, toads can't breed underground either, a fact that puts a certain premium on surface time. And the process gets a bit complicated in deserts, where there is no standing water and the spadefoots must use temporary pools. As a result, they have given up a regular breeding calendar and may breed at any time of year that is both warm enough and wet enough. Apparently either the sound or the vibration of raindrops drumming on the earth overhead stimulates the toads' hormones and gets the whole reproductive process going. The male spadefoot may well be the only animal in nature that is sexually excited by heavy rain.

The resulting tadpoles have the distinction of being the fastest to mature of any anurans, sometimes taking as little as nine days from egg to toadlet. They are generally in a race for their lives with the process of evaporation: the hotter the sun, the faster they develop—but the hotter the sun, the more quickly their watery habitat disappears. They

**Soldier and Prostitute
with Frog Brooch**
*Arthur Boyd (b. 1920, Australia)
Reed pen and ink
26.3 x 36.8 cm., 1943
Purchased 1966; reproduced by
permission of the National Gallery
of Victoria, Melbourne, Australia,
and of Arthur Boyd*

do not always win this race. Some of the more poignant toad photographs I have seen show hundreds of dead tadpoles lying in the mud at the bottom of dried-out pools. In some cases they may even have cooperated to scoop out a deeper hole in the pond bottom, where the remaining puddle would last a few hours longer.

The tadpoles have developed a few special tricks to promote rapid development. For one thing, they may form large groups to stir up the bottom mud with their tails and find food. For another, some of them may turn cannibal. These individuals will grow much faster and metamorphose sooner than their fellows, which is nature's way of making it more likely that at least a few new toads will be produced.

(Strangely enough, these same toads apparently exhibit no cannibalistic behavior when they reach adulthood.) When all else fails, it seems that the remains of dried tadpoles left in a pool will somehow, perhaps chemically, promote quicker metamorphosis of the tads in the following year, who may, if necessary, be ready to begin toad life when they reach the approximate size of houseflies.

By the end of their first summer, most spadefoots will have reached a third to a half of their adult size, and probably by the end of their second summer most will be sexually mature. However, as Bragg records, they may show some interest in sex even as adolescents:

> I have recently made one minor observation on the sexual behavior of juveniles of the Plains Spadefoot. The container occupied by 35 or 40 of these which were still quite small and immature became flooded during a rain. A short time later I found these animals attempting to clasp each other as they floated on the water. They were very active, swimming about in mated pairs much like the adults, with some of them squeaking their high pitched protesting notes when clasped. This behavior must have been a sort of sexual play resulting from the stimulus of flooding which had called forth the clasping instinct as in adults.   [Bragg, 1965: 94-95]

The Midwife Toad

On 23 September 1926, a brilliant Viennese scientist named Paul Kammerer put a bullet through his head. His suicide convinced many who until then had been in doubt that his enemies were right in claiming that the results of his celebrated experiments with the midwife toad *(Alytes obstetricans)* had been faked. Since then Kammerer has been held up to generations of college science students as an object lesson in the futility of scientific fraud: in science, we believe, the truth will out.

Only decades later was the Kammerer story reexamined in all its intricate complexity by Arthur Koestler, in his brilliant monograph entitled *The Case of the Midwife Toad* (1972). Koestler approaches the case of Kammerer as an objective observer, reviews the mountain of evidence with painstaking care, and finds for the defendant.

The midwife toad of southern Europe gets its name from its distinctive mating behavior. It lays its eggs on land; once the double string of eggs are laid and fertilized, the male pulls them off the female's hind legs and entwines them around his own hips and thighs. There they remain for several days, while the now solitary male goes about his business as usual, except for occasionally dipping the eggs in water to keep them from drying out. When the eggs are ready to hatch, he deposits them in a vacant pond, after which the tads are free to develop in more normal anuran fashion.

The peculiarity of this species that was to become so significant is

MALE OF MIDWIFE FROG
WITH CHAINS OF EGGS
from Richard Lydekker's The
New Natural History *(six
vols.), n.d.
Reproduced from* Animal Art
in the Public Domain
*edited by Harold H. Hart
Copyright 1983 by Hart
Publishing Company, New York
Photo by Judith DeGraaff*

the fact that the male (except in certain rare instances) fails to develop the so-called "nuptial pads" normally exhibited by other species during the breeding season. These pads are patches of thickened and darkened skin with tiny bristles, occurring on the front feet, which enable male toads to hang onto slippery females in the water. Presumably the male midwife has none because he can get a good enough grip on the dry, rough skin of his partner without them.

What Kammerer did, over a period of several years, was to force several successive generations of *Alytes* to breed in water—and what he found was that by the third such generation the males were exhibiting nuptial pads. This seemed to be evidence that the Lamarckian evolutionists (of whom Kammerer was one) were right in supposing that acquired characteristics could be passed on through the genes. Actually, Kammerer himself never put much stock in this evidence, which he pointed out could be simply the reemergence of an earlier feature of the toad that had disappeared through disuse. He regarded certain other experiments he had done with sea squirts as far more conclusive.

But the Darwinians, who believed that evolution worked only through random mutation and subsequent survival of the fittest, were riding the crest of their new orthodoxy, and had become obsessed with those nuptial pads on the midwife toad. The pads, they claimed, were in the wrong place; perhaps, they implied, the pads had been transplanted onto Kammerer's toads from another species. A few halfhearted attempts were made to duplicate Kammerer's experiments, but they were careless and did not even consider Kammerer's own notes and comments. They failed. Kammerer was asked to furnish microscopic photographs; he did. He was invited to give a demonstration lecture at Cambridge; he did. Many remained skeptical, but no one could disprove the genuineness of those pads.

It wasn't until a few years later that the Darwinians got the break they were looking for; an examination of the last remaining preserved specimen of midwife toad in Vienna revealed that its front feet had been injected with India ink. It was at this point that Kammerer apparently gave up in despair and took his own life, thereby ensuring that his name would live in infamy.

But Koestler does not accept the suicide as proof of Kammerer's guilt. Those pads were really there, he believes, and the ink was injected later, either by an overzealous lab assistant—perhaps to restore the faded color in the aging specimen—or by someone out to deliberately discredit Kammerer. Incredibly enough, no serious effort has yet been made to duplicate Kammerer's experiments with the midwife toad, which might finally settle the matter. In the meanwhile, as Koestler points out, pure Darwinism seems less and less adequate, even on the basis of mathematical odds alone, to explain the origin of species, and recently some scientists have suggested that there may be circumstances under which RNA, the genetic "messenger substance," may affect DNA, the basic genetic "blueprint"; in other words, Lamarckian evolution may have some limited validity. Thus there may still be hope for the eventual exoneration of a great scientist and ardent bufophile.

TOAD MUSIC & MATING

Caught in that sensual music all neglect
Monuments of unaging intellect.

W. B. Yeats, "Sailing to Byzantium"

Before the earliest evolutionary adaptations, when the toad's amphibian ancestors first crawled out of the water, they must have entered a very quiet world. There probably was little more than the sound of the wind in the reeds and ferns until the voice of the toad—earth's primeval music—was heard in the land.

"Some say the lark and loathed toad changed eyes./O now I would they had changed voices too," says Shakespeare's Juliet. The lark's morning song serves as a sort of alarm clock at that point in the play, but since morning means that she must part from her Romeo, the song sounds to Juliet like the unpleasant croaking of a toad.

In thus insulting the little amphibian, Juliet reveals the ignorance of her youth. In the first place, the calls of some species of toads are as melodious as those of any bird. Secondly, unlike birds, toads make their music with genuine vocal cords; they are in a class with the best. Dyed-in-the-wool herpetologists take as much listening pleasure in a record of toad and frog calls—such as Kellogg and Allen's *Voices of the Night*—

as does any ornithologist in his taped bird songs.

In pitch, toad voices cover a wide musical range: the low pitch of Fowler's toad or some of the spadefoots rivals the profound bass of the bullfrog, while the Southern toad definitely qualifies as a soprano and the little oak toad may reach nearly three octaves above middle C [Potter: 147].

> At ease he sits upon the pool,
>   And, void of fuss or trouble,
> Makes vesper music fit for kings
>   From out an empty bubble:
>
> A long-drawn-out and tolling cry,
>   That drifts above the chorus
> Of shriller voices from the marsh
>   That April nights send o'er us;
> A tender monotone of song
>   With vernal longings blending,
> That rises from the ponds and pools,
>   And seems at times unending;
>
> A linked chain of bubbling notes,
>   When birds have ceased their calling,
> That lulls the ear with soothing sound
>   Like voice of water falling.
> It is the knell of winter dead;
>   Good-by, his icy fetter.
> Blessings on thy warty head:
>   No bird could do it better.
>
> John Burroughs, "The Song of the Toad"

Attempts to describe the quality of toad sounds have sometimes drawn upon comparisons with birds. The call of the African toad *Bufo regularis*, for example, has been said to resemble that of the blue crane, while that of *Bufo xeros* is like the hoot of a large owl [Tandy et al.: 1, 6], and the natterjack has been called "the Thursley thrush" and "the Birkdale nightingale" [Beebee: viii].

The Yosemite toad recalls the courting song of the Texas nighthawk [J. Grinnell and T. I. Storer, cited in Wright and Wright: 163] while both the Western toad and the oak toad sound like young

OAK TOAD
Bufo quercicus, n.d.
Terence Shortt
watercolor on paper, 9.9 x 17.8 cm.
Collection of Martina R. Norelli
Photo by Gene Young

chickens peeping. The spadefoots, somewhat less musical, emit sharp grunts that may sound like explosive quacks [Smith: 34] or the coarse complaints of young crows [Behler and King: 365].

But as the scientists inform us, toads do not always sound like birds. The Mexican burrowing toad emits a loud guttural moan [Behler and King: 361], and "a chorus of them sounds like a shipload of seasick landlubbers" [Goin et al.: 227]. The sheep toad bleats like a lost lamb, while Woodhouse's toad sounds more like a sheep with a cold [Behler and King: 398]. The cliff toad and the green toad sound like crickets [Smith: 28; Behler and King: 390]; the Western spadefoot has "a rolling trill like the purr of a cat" [Behler and King: 364]. Other species emit nasal quonks, deep moans, faint buzzes, shrill liquid trills, whistled wheets, warbling chirps, raspy snores, metallic vibratos, weak low-pitched toots, short squeaks, doglike barks, deep low-volume honks, or explosive grunts.

And this is only the beginning of the devastation wrought upon the scientists by the poetic muse. The Western spadefoot, we are told, has a "vibrant metallic trill like running a fingernail along the stiff teeth of a large comb." The Texas toad sounds like "a high-pitched riveting machine"; the Eastern green toad sounds its "shrill trill, almost with the insistence of an irate policeman's whistle"; and the giant toad's slow, low-pitched trill is "suggestive of the exhaust noise of a distant tractor" [Conant: 302, 313, 314, 315].

The volume of sound generated by a pondful of singing males, of one or more species, may, for the human ear, approach the threshold of pain—"a great caterwauling," as "noisy as a steam calliope" [Wright and Wright: 126]. At a greater distance, however, the sound is not so overwhelming: a distant chorus of giant toads may remind one of "an idling diesel engine" [Behler and King: 393].

Toads Breeding, Thumb Swelling

1
They start again,
the toads, bilious whistle
worse than cicadas, nighttime screech
toneless as faucet water. Turn it off,
I mutter, harried from hammering studs all day.
I deserve quiet air cool as justice.
Thick-lidded judges, they nail my eyes
and brain together. All night I hear
the drop on drop of seamless screaming.

2
The tadpoles gather
at the mouths of fishes, kiss,
then scurry toward my bruised thumb.
The shed is up. My sweat plunks their water
like oil. I am full of song, backroad ballads
Hank Snow traveled. They squiggle away,
blackened stones thumped from air. A cairn
rises; I wail on. Oh, all day I drift
through cotton fields light as whey.

3
Now, rumps in mud,

we hunker at pond's edge
eyeing cracks and dry algae. Toads,
I mutter, we survived. Let's rest.
In my dream of swamps, fog, stars disappearing,
toads squat on tree stumps, peat moss smokes.
There, I say, imagine next season.
Nailheads stare back. My thumb plops
into sealant. No one hears it, I know,
in Texas in Sarasota in Muncie, Indiana.

Philip Raisor

A few of the more larklike amphibian soloists are the Yosemite toad, whose mating call is "a pleasant vibrato of 10–20 notes, repeated often" [Smith: 40], and the American toad, abundant in the northeastern United States, whose melodious trill, lasting between six and thirty seconds, is surely "one of the most pleasant sounds of early spring" [Conant: 307]. The sound, it has been suggested, may be imitated by humans "whistling in a low monotone with drops of water held between the lips" [F. Overton, cited in Wright and Wright: 142]. The California toad lacks the vocal sacs that enable sweet toad singers to resonate properly, but he seems to make the most of what nature has given him: "the male has a friendly chuckle, which it gives at times while mated" [Wright and Wright: 154].

Most toad music is related, directly or indirectly, to the grand reproductive enterprise. A very few anuran species, such as those that live in noisy streams where they probably could not make themselves heard anyway, seem to lack a mating call altogether. Some very isolated species, having little need to sing, seem to have lost their voice: males and females alike simply know where to find the breeding pools, and there are no strange neighboring species to cause confusion in pairing off. Another minority comprises species with voices but without vocal sacs, who can only emit faint sounds.

In the typical toad situation, though, the males do have vocal sacs. Without opening their mouths, they force air back and forth from the lungs to the vocal sacs across a complex laryngeal structure consisting of two delicate vocal cords, modified by cushions of tissue to the front and paired folds of tissue on the back. Having migrated to the mating pools in early spring, the males put all this vocal equipment to work in

the breeding chorus, whose sound may carry as much as a half mile or more, guiding the egg-heavy females to the right pools, the right species (each species has a distinctive call), and possibly even to the right males. Some evidence suggests not only that the deeper voices of the larger males are more attractive to females, but also that larger males may seek out and defend sites on land or in water whose cooler temperatures will help them get the most out of their bass range. The mating calls seem useful in marking out such territories.

But in this, as in all areas of toad behavior, there are wide variations among the various species. Males may call from shallow water, deeper water, or underwater; they may call from caves, from shorelines, even from underground. Or they may not call at all—and yet somehow the business gets done.

Mating calls are not the only toad sounds. A friend of mine, poet Albert Glover, was walking in his garden last summer when he heard a sort of scream, as though someone were in trouble and crying out for help. After looking high and low, he found the source of the cry beneath some squash leaves at his feet: it was a small toad being swallowed by

CERAMIC POTS
Rachael Mellors
1986
Photo by Rachael Mellors

a snake. Now Albert faced a dilemma: was this a natural process, not to be interfered with, or was this a summons, a glimpse behind nature's veil? A line from *Paradise Lost* seemed to provide the solution—"Her seed shall bruise [the serpent's] head." Slowly Glover applied pressure to the small snake's neck with his heel until it opened its mouth and released the toad, which hopped off, unharmed, into the garden rubble.

What Glover had responded to is usually referred to as the "distress call." It is thought to work by startling would-be predators and causing them to drop their prey, although in this case it didn't seem to be working very well.

Other people claim to have heard anuran noises like "friendly chuckles" or "low grunting sounds as if of contentment," and it seems clear that many anurans, outside their breeding seasons, sing before rainfall; but the scientific literature focuses on those calls associated with sex. Lorcher, for example, finds that the fire-bellied toad has five different calls: "the normal mating call, the modified mating call, the clasping call and the release calls of first and second order" [Lorcher: 84].

A toad's "release call" is usually a short chirp or "chuckle" accompanied by a vibration of its lower body. The call is an important one in the toad repertoire, since a male toad is an intensely sexy toad during the breeding season:

> All he knows . . . is that he wants to get his arms round something, and if you offer him a stick, or even your finger, he will cling to it with surprising strength and take a long time to discover that it is not a female toad. Frequently one comes upon shapeless masses of ten or twenty toads rolling over and over in the water, one clinging to another without distinction of sex.
>
> George Orwell, "Some Thoughts on the Common Toad"

Sometimes the female gets drowned in the melee, and a male may embrace the dead body for several days. So strong is the mating drive that some males have even been discovered grasping attractive lumps of mud along the shoreline. The release call can prevent some of the problems caused by such sheer intensity. Used by a male toad, it tells another male that he is mounted on the wrong sex. Females use it to get free once they have laid their eggs and wish to leave the pond in peace. And, since these calls also vary with each different species, they may be effective in preventing crossbreeding.

Looked at from the female's point of view, breeding seems a compulsive and potentially dangerous business, to which she is driven by the irrepressible urge to get her eggs laid. As she responds to the sound of the male chorus and makes her heavy way down to the pool, she may be boarded some distance away and ridden into the water, or she may be accosted at the shoreline; once in the water, she may be drowned in a male wrestling bout, or suffer fungal infection in the armpits from prolonged contact with the male's nuptial pads.

However, the female's role is not always as passive as all that. In some species the males establish clearly defined territories, and she may approach the partner of her choice. She may be helped in locating the dominant male by the nature of the chorus itself, in which the sequence of the singers reflects their order of power. Or she may seek out an individual singer whose size is revealed by the lower pitch and greater intensity of his song. In some species, she may have a certain amount of leisure to swim around and investigate the possibilities, as the males will respond to her only when they are actually touched.

> Some very interesting recent work with common toads *(Bufo bufo)* has shown that a female seized by a male much smaller than herself might deliberately move into an area with many free males swimming about. Males of the common toad are . . . aggressive . . . and will attempt to displace those already paired. Now, when a male in amplexus is attacked by another he emits a characteristic short croak, the pitch of which varies according to his size . . . hence the incumbent animal is forced to reveal something of his size (and therefore strength) to would-be attackers. Experiments have shown that this does indeed lead to more vigorous assault and the virtually inevitable replacement of the small animal by one of a size more likely to effect efficient fertilization.   [Beebee: 72]

The most usual toad reproduction process may be described as follows: the male mounts the female in the water, grasping her either at the armpits or around the middle with his front legs (the exact position of amplexus depends on the species), thus putting his cloacal

opening, or venter, in close proximity to hers. After a period of time ranging from a few minutes to a few hours, she begins laying her eggs, which may number up to thirty thousand and which emerge as a pair of long strings. Each release of eggs is signaled by a body vibration, which triggers the release of sperm at the right moment: sperm and egg unite in the water by chemical attraction. The eggs are covered with a thin membrane that swells into a jellylike substance when it contacts the water, thereby forming a protective coating. The two toads move about a bit, spreading eggs on the pond bottom or entwining the strings around underwater vegetation. The eggs are laid within a few hours' time, after which the female returns to land; the males remain at the pool for the length of the breeding season.

The tadpoles hatch within a few days. Typically they breathe through gills and eat vegetable matter, for which they have several rows of tiny teeth and a relatively long digestive tract. Toward the end of their development as tads, which may take as little as two weeks or as much as two years, that spectacular metamorphosis occurs which so intrigues schoolchildren: the hind legs sprout, the gills change to lungs, the mouth parts change, the digestive tract shortens, the body shape alters, the front legs appear, and the toadlet is ready to leave the water. He can live for a while by reabsorbing his own tail. At some point when he is between one and four years old, he will become sexually mature and return, perhaps to the same pond, to begin the game anew.

This is the basic anuran pattern, but there are many interesting variations. As in the case of the midwife toad, some species breed on land, the eggs requiring special care (in these cases far fewer eggs are usually laid). The male may babysit eggs wound round his hind legs, or he may incubate them in his vocal sacs; the female may incubate them in her mouth or even in her stomach, whose normal digestive activities are temporarily suspended. The "tailed toad" *(Ascaphus truei)* of the Pacific coast actually has a section of its cloaca protruding, with which the males can fertilize eggs inside the female—a useful device for successful fertilization in fast-flowing mountain streams where egg or sperm might be swept away. Unfortunately the African live-bearing toads (Nectaphrynoides), who could really use such a "tail," have failed to develop one. They breed on land, and fertilization is internal, so they must rely on a perfect alignment of venters for the sperm to be able to enter the female; as many as one hundred eggs may be incubated to maturity in her oviducts, later to be born alive as fully formed toadlets. Technically, though, these toads are not really viviparous, since the mother does not directly nourish the embryos but only provides a place inside her body for them to grow up in.

Perhaps the most bizarre breeding pattern of all is that of the Surinam toad, a strange looking, tongueless anuran who never leaves the water. The male grasps the female around the lower body, and together they perform a series of loop-the-loops, consisting of a half-roll and a half-forward somersault [Rabb: 44]. Near the top of each

FEMALE SURINAM WATER-TOAD, SHOWING YOUNG IN THEIR CELLS
from Richard Lydekker's The New Natural History *(six vols.), n.d.*
Reproduced from Animal Art in the Public Domain
edited by Harold H. Hart
Copyright 1983 by Hart Publishing Company, New York
Photo by Judith DeGraaff

loop, while upside down, she lays a few eggs, which are caught in a
skinfold on his belly. As the couple comes right side up, he fertilizes and
presses them to the female's back, where they catch and stick (if they

miss, they are lost). Once these Ferris-wheel rotations are over, she may have fifty or a hundred eggs sticking to her. Over a period of a few days these eggs slowly sink into the female's back, where pits form to receive them and they are sealed in by the eggs' own membrane. Fully formed young emerge from these pockets a few months later, perhaps partly forced out by internal maternal pressure [Rabb: 45].

Orgy With Toads
(Will, Flora, Phil, Nora, Nil, Laura)

WILL

Flora and I know hardly anything:
Both of us were busy listening
To Martistaag's atonal Opera
Bufo *on our tinny pornograph,*
Thinking no evil: suddenly we heard
A jagged, tearing noise—

FLORA

    When they appeared,
We said, Harmless harmless. No one thought to
Page the Anarch, no one thought we ought to.
Phil and I were holding dress rehearsal
For the Second Coming, when we noticed—toads!
Toads all around us in the darksome woods,
A veritable plethora of toads.

PHIL

Think of green pebbles, bits of polished jade—
Nora and I were playing Masquerade.
The toads were tiny, very, very tiny,
And hopped all over us, the little devils.
No one thought to summon the Master of Revels,
Or thought of the old legends of wartiness,
Or even of the proverbial saying,
"Ants at a picnic, toads at an orgy."

NORA

Nil and I were doing needlepoint
When suddenly I felt the needles slip—

"Look!" he said, and "Look, look!" His fingertip
Seemed to be palping, at a certain distance,
What I can only think of as an absence,
But an absence which was more than just an absence—
It was as though, in the imagined fabric
Of the really real, a rent had opened up, and
From an area of pure negation
There came an outpouring, which, in retrospect,
One might have called a not-being-there of toads.
Later, I saw them.

NIL

Nora was nowhere.
Laura and I were busy playing Doctor.
I was the Doctor, I made Laura drink
A liquor thick as tar, black as ink.
I turned the largest toad into a Prince.

LAURA

Unsavory japes were made at their expense,
Vulgar buffoonery, ribald scheming.
Will and I were doing our blaspheming:
I was the Chalice, he the Minister.
He paused, then said, "There's something . . . faintly . . .   sinister—"
The toads were thick as toadstools on the grass:
No ears to speak of, eyes like bits of glass,
Wind-swollen bellies, flagrantly distended;
Will said, "Disgusting. Vulgar. Post-lapsarian."
We called for the Authoritarian,
And shortly afterward, the Orgy ended.

                                        Charles Martin

TOAD NAVIGATION

The Little Toads Start Out To See The World

The world is a wonderful great big place
And in it the young must roam
To learn what their elders have long since learned—
There's never a place like home.

It had been some time since Peter Rabbit had visited the Smiling Pool to watch the pollywogs. But one cloudy morning he happened to think of them and decided that he would run over there and see how they were getting along. So off he started, lipperty-lipperty-lip. He wondered if those pollywog children of Old Mr. Toad would be much changed. The last time he saw them some of them had just begun to grow legs, although they still had long tails.

He had almost reached the Smiling Pool when great big drops of rain began to splash down. And with those first raindrops something funny happened. Anyway, it seemed funny to Peter. Right away he was surrounded by tiny little Toads. Everywhere he looked he saw Toads, tiny little Toads just like Old Mr. Toad, only so tiny that one could have sat comfortably on a ten-cent piece and still had plenty of room.

Peter's big eyes grew round with surprise as he stared. Where had they all come from so suddenly? A minute before he hadn't seen a single one, and now he could hardly move without stepping on one. It seemed, it really seemed, as if each raindrop turned into a tiny Toad the instant it struck the ground. Of course, Peter knew that that couldn't be, but it was very puzzling. And all those little Toads were *bravely hopping along as if they were bound for some particular place.*

Peter watched them for a few minutes, then he once more started for the Smiling Pool. On the very bank whom should he meet but Old Mr. Toad. He looked rather thin, and his back was to the Smiling Pool. Yes, Sir, he was hopping away from the Smiling Pool where he had been all the spring, singing in the great chorus. Peter was almost as surprised to see him as he had been to see the little Toads, but just then he was most interested in those little Toads.

"Good morning, Old Mr. Toad," said Peter in his most polite manner. "Can you tell me where all these little Toads came from?"

"Certainly," replied Old Mr. Toad. "They came from the Smiling Pool, of course. Where did you suppose they came from?"

"I—I didn't know. There wasn't one to be seen, and then it began to rain, and right away they were everywhere. It—it almost seemed as if they had rained down out of the sky."

Old Mr. Toad chuckled. "They've got good sense, if I must say it about my own children," said he. "They know that wet weather is the only weather for Toads to travel in. They left the Smiling Pool in the night while it was damp and comfortable, and then, when the sun came up, they hid, like sensible children, under anything they could find, sticks, stones, pieces of bark, grass. The minute this shower came up, they knew it was good traveling weather and out they popped."

"But what did they leave the Smiling Pool for?" Peter asked.

"To see the Great World," replied Old Mr. Toad. "Foolish, very foolish of them, but they would do it. I did the same thing myself when I was their age. Couldn't stop me any more than I could stop them. They don't know when they're well off, but young folks never do. Fine weather, isn't it?"

Thornton Burgess, The Adventures of Old Mr. Toad

Toadlets are likely to stay pretty close to their home pond for several days following their mass exodus from the water. Some of them may still have bits of tail to reabsorb, but perhaps the most important thing is getting their land legs and getting oriented. In many cases toads seem to return to the same pond as breeding adults some two or three years later, and, since laboratory experiments have not revealed much capacity for memory in the toad, the great mystery is how they manage it. Once a breeding chorus has begun, of course, the pond should be pretty easy to find for any toad within hearing, and it seems clear that females especially respond to that sensual music. But how does the first toad find the pond, and what about those out of hearing range?

One theory is that the toadlets imprint the pond's odor and then follow their noses when the proper time comes, and some lab experiments show that toad sex hormones, active during the breeding season, do in fact sensitize toads to the odors of their home ponds. What remains hard to explain by the smell theory is how a large number of toads can find the same pond, in the absence of chorusing, from all directions at once—which means that some must approach from downwind. Some experimenters who have been willing to go so far as to slash olfactory nerves have had mixed results: some found that the resulting anosmic toads could still find their way around, while others simply produced some very confused toads. Evidently, most toads do not move by smell alone.

A second theory is that toads orient spatially on a "Y-axis," perpendicular to the shoreline of a home pond or other landmark, and thereafter navigate by celestial clues in relation to that pattern. The Western toad was found, in a typical experiment, to possess a sun compass and biological clock: toads captured and later released in a laboratory setting in which only the sky was visible, generally set off in what would have been the proper direction to bring them back to the shores of their home ponds. But again, other experiments seem to show that at least some species of toads are able to find their way around with no celestial aid, either under totally overcast skies, or when blinded.

Most herpetologists now seem to agree that toads probably use a combination of orienting mechanisms, not only for finding their home ponds, but also for getting around their home ranges: sight, sound, smell, and celestial navigation may all be used, separately or in combination, depending on conditions (and subject to possible species variations). There may even be some as yet undiscovered mechanism at work. A migratory instinct, like that of birds, seems very unlikely: if displaced more than a few miles from their home range, toads do not seem to make any effort to return, but simply relocate. On the other hand, toad forebears must have had some wanderlust in order to populate most of the planet—and no one has yet explained why many thousands of toads turned up in a body at Grand Forks, Minnesota, a few decades ago, in an incident reminiscent of the biblical plague of frogs.

It seems a peculiar whim of nature that this small, slow-moving creature should be a wanderer upon the face of the earth, but many

TOAD'S HOME

toads, either whole species or particular individuals, are in fact highly mobile. (Hence the love Kenneth Grahame's Mr. Toad had for traveling in the fast lane may be more appropriate than it initially appears to be.) A particular toad's home range has been shown to be as much as a square mile, and a displaced toad may return to that range from more than a mile away. One Carolina toad, hopping aerobically, covered almost half a mile in a single rainy night [Bogert, 1947: 11]. Other individuals, though, seem contented with a much smaller range. Perhaps they are more timid; or perhaps they are simply more fortunate in having suitable shelters to hole up in during the day, and sufficiently productive feeding stations to use at night.

TOAD'S HOME
Charles Doyle
Henry E. Huntington Library
and Art Gallery

TOAD THE HUNTER

Mrs. Perkins . . . saluted . . . as the toad catches flies—so quick that few saw the operation.

WILLIAM T. THOMPSON, *CHRONICLES OF PINEVILLE*

Despite its slow and clumsy gait, the speed and accuracy of the toad's tongue make it a formidable hunter. Many observers of feeding toads report seeing nothing except the sudden and mysterious disappearance of insects in the toad's immediate vicinity. They bear witness to the amazing speed of the tongue-flip, which has been shown to take, from opening of mouth to impact on prey, about sixteen one-thousandths of a second [for the American toad; Dean: 43]. Retraction of the tongue occurs at about the same lightning speed, so that an insect crawling happily along might well find itself inside a toad's mouth and about to be swallowed in something like three one-hundredths of a second. One study shows that the toad's tongue-flip depends on the abrupt stiffening of two masses of rod-shaped muscles in the tongue, "to form a lever system that flips the fleshy tip toward the prey as a medieval ballista or trebuchet flipped a boulder, or as one flips the strings on a mop" [Gans and Gorniak:1335].

Traditional toad lore has it that toads feed only on moving prey.

A toad will point, not unlike a bird dog, in the direction of an insect moving within its field of vision, and stalk it slowly, stopping when it stops, until within range—then follows a final lunge forward, accompanied by that astonishing tongue thrust. If an insect has the wit to sit still long enough, as has been observed more than once, a toad loses interest and moves on.

To test the Southern toad's visual perceptions in feeding, Walter and Francis Kaess experimented with a motorized Lazy Susan, its rim decorated with small pellets of hamburger. When the wheel was still, the toads showed little interest in the burgers; some of them took a long look, but not one opened its mouth. As soon as it began to spin, however, the toads approached and began to feed.

> Five or six toads, each oriented toward the center of the disk, knocking off pellets of hamburger (accuracy, 95 percent) like sharp-shooters potting ducks in a shooting gallery, [made] a spectacular sight.   [Kaess and Kaess: 953]

Even more interesting was what happened when a toad happened to crawl or hop onto the revolving disk; at this point the hamburger pellets, in relation to the toad, would no longer seem to be moving. When toads in this position continued to feed, the experimenters theorized that an illusion of motion must have been induced by the apparent movement of the background, just as humans feel themselves to be moving while actually sitting in a stationary train, if the train on an adjacent track begins to pull out [Kaess and Kaess: 953].

While vision is undoubtedly the key sense in toad's feeding, it has been found that toads will eat in extremely dim light, even in absolute darkness. Blind toads are alerted by the sound of prey movements but apparently do not stalk prey, and eat only those insects that actually bump into them [Martof: 439]. The puzzle for many early experimenters was why the toad did not rely more heavily on its sense of smell. As Jonathan Risser pointed out as early as 1914, "A chambered nasal cavity of considerable magnitude supplied extensively with olfactory epithelium and adequate connections with the central nervous system, predicate functional activity of the sense organ" [Risser: 648]. In other words, the toad has a good nose, so why doesn't he use it?

The answer, as several recent experimenters have found, is that he does. The work of Elizabeth Shinn and Jim Dole with the Western toad shows that the sense of smell, by itself, can stimulate feeding responses. These toads showed a pronounced partiality for the odor bouquet of their favorite insect, the cricket—so intense that they would snuff the ground like miniature bloodhounds, follow the scent, and flip out their tongues at its apparent source, even when no actual cricket, or moving prey of any kind, was in sight [Shinn and Dole, 1979b: 275].

Just as is the case with toad orientation, the more that is known about toad feeding, the more complex the behavior seems to be; and for almost every general pattern that emerges, there seem to be exceptions. After many years of intensive observation of about a dozen species of *Bufo* and *Scaphiopus*, Arthur Bragg reported that while most toads orient toward a moving insect, crawl within range, and only strike when the insect resumes movement, a few will strike even if the insect remains motionless. Some toads will even strike at the first appearance of an insect, such as a flying moth, without any orientation or stalking behavior whatever [Bragg, 1957: 190]. Indeed, it seems that toad responses to objects arriving by air are perforce less deliberate than normal. One observer reported seeing a toad "sitting beneath a mulberry tree and ingesting the berries as they fell from the tree and rolled and bounced along the ground" [Bragg, 1957: 190]. Another found a fatal epidemic among giant toads in Hawaii who were spearing the falling blossoms from strychnine trees. One large toad even swallowed a ping pong ball that was bounced toward it, perhaps because it resembled a wounded flying insect [Oliver: 199].

Mysteriously, Bragg never observed a toad eat another toad, even one that was the right size for prey: a large toad might orient briefly to the movement of a toadlet, but never pursued it. This seems odd, both since spadefoot tadpoles sometimes turn cannibal, and since toads' brother amphibians, the frogs, are notorious devourers of the offspring of other species of *Rana*, or even their own [Bragg, 1957: 189–190].

Taylor Alexander's experience with some twenty giant toads in his Florida backyard brings to light some other unusual feeding details:

> The first observations on feeding behavior were made on
> several large toads that began to come each night to the dog's

plate in the backyard and wait until the dog had eaten all the canned dog food it wanted. They would then move in and gulp down the remainder. They would locate and eat small scattered pieces that had fallen into the grass. It was thought initially that insects might be coming to the meat and might be involved as the real attractant, but none was observed. When the dog was kept indoors and a can of dog meat emptied onto the plate or onto the grass, the toads would come immediately to the meat. They would sit very still in front of it a few minutes and then first one then another would lunge at the meat and bite out big mouthfuls. This would continue until the food was completely gone and they had gotten all the scattered pieces. It appeared a "peck order" was in operation with the smaller toads remaining in the background until they were allowed to feed by the larger toads.

Later a larger group began to stay around a mulch pile in the garden where plant materials and garbage from the kitchen were put. At first the toads were seen mostly at night, but gradually they began to appear during the day. In fact, they eventually would come out of hiding anytime that fresh garbage was brought out regardless of the time of day or night. As in the case with the meat, they would move in close to the food, sit there a moment, and suddenly lunge forward to pick up or tear off bite-size pieces . . . .

They would lunge at and grab pieces such as lettuce leaves and carrot peelings, and if parts hung out of their mouths, they would work them into their mouths by using their front feet. In some cases it would take considerable time before they could manage to swallow all of the material. Large lettuce leaves frequently were torn into smaller pieces by their lunge-biting action. Soft avocado meat was simply bitten into by lunging. None of this food would be moving by wind action and no insects were involved. The toads became very tame and allowed extremely close observation and photography at all times. At times certain individuals would display extreme aggressiveness and push others away from the food . . . .

The behavior of these toads appears very unusual when compared to most statements on feeding in the literature. They definitely fed extensively in an omnivorous manner over a period of time and did so during all hours of the day as well as at night. They took nonmoving material as food and seemed to become acclimated to the sounds, sight, and/or odor of food being placed where they could get to it. This was obvious as they could be seen hopping in from distances of 20 feet or more from places where they had been hiding.

[Alexander: 255–256, 257, 258]

Even toads with more normal eating habits have often been found to have pebbles or other indigestible matter in their stomachs, presumably taken in along with prey, or perhaps because it happened to be moving or rolling in such a way as to be mistaken for some insect. Since a toad can be fooled in this way, and since, lacking teeth, it cannot chew its food but swallows objects whole and very quickly, how can eating mistakes be corrected?

Many researchers have noted a lack of good eating sense in small toadlets, whose eyes are sometimes bigger than their stomachs. Large insects may be flapped, but are in no real danger from these diminutive gluttons. More interesting is Jeffrey Dean's work with two species of adult toads *(Bufo americanus* and *Bufo marinus)* and bombardier beetles [1980]. These beetles have a potent chemical defense when attacked—an almost instantaneous fiery explosion from their tail ends. The toads are fast enough to mouth these beetles, but not fast enough to actually swallow them before they begin blasting away. The giant toad *(Bufo marinus)* generally does get the beetles down before they begin firing, perhaps because its capacious mouth puts no unusual stresses upon the prey, who may be more fascinated than threatened by the whole process. Even the occasional blast in the mouth or stomach seldom seems to cause the giant toad much discomfort—at any rate not enough to prevent him from promptly attacking the next beetle that comes into view. The smaller American toad has a more difficult time of it, mostly because swallowing the beetle is a major operation. By the time the beetle feels itself pinched into the back of the toad's mouth, being forced toward the short esophagus by the bottom side of the toad's retracted eyeballs, it gets aroused and begins to fire at will. Dean reports the result:

During strikes at bombardier beetles, the toad's eyes barely closed before both eyes and mouth suddenly popped open and the tongue curled forward, still carrying the beetle . . . attached by its back upside down, with legs flailing.

[Dean: 45]

EUROPEAN COMMON TOAD
from Animals
edited by Jim Harter
Copyright 1979 by
Dover Publications, Inc.
New York
Photo by Judith DeGraaff

At this point the toad's own sticky tongue became a liability, as the fiery intruder could not easily be discharged, but had to be scraped free—either by pulling the tongue past a partly closed upper jaw, or by "flicking a foreleg rapidly past the side and front of the mouth" [Dean: 45].

Having got rid of the beetle, the toad (1) showed its aversion and (2) practiced a kind of studied avoidance:

> The most common behavior was simply to back away from the beetle. If the beetle moved towards the toad, the avoidance became more active: the toad either continued backing away or waved one of its forelegs towards the beetle as though brushing it away. Also common was a behavior, which I will refer to as "mouth airing," in which the toad briefly reopened its mouth with the tongue bulging at the tip of the lower jaw or extending in a curl out of the mouth. In extreme cases, the lower jaw fluttered slightly up and down several times before the tongue retracted and the mouth again closed . . . . Other

behaviors associated with rejections included repeated swallowing motions together with eye retraction, lifting a foreleg and brushing it past the eye which then blinked, and exaggerated swallowing and eye closure at the approach of a beetle.

[Dean: 45]

Evidently the beetle was able to make a strong impression on *Bufo americanus*, though not a lasting one—most toads were ready to repeat the whole process if offered another beetle several days later.

One of the reasons for this, apart from a weak memory, may be that the toads were occasionally successful in eating bombardier beetles without setting off explosive reactions. On other occasions, the beetles apparently resorted to violence only after arrival in the toad's stomach, which led to repeated "mouth airings" in one toad, while another toad "emitted trains of muted chirps and rapidly puffed its abdomen in and out, a behavior normally associated with defense"[Dean: 47]. The most extreme reaction observed by Dean was in a toad that had swallowed one beetle and rejected a second shortly thereafter. Having most probably been blasted both in the stomach and the mouth, this toad must have been suffering a bad case of acid indigestion, and within a few minutes resorted to regurgitation. The vomiting consisted in turning the stomach inside out through the mouth to empty it, then reswallowing the stomach. In view of the number of insects with chemical defenses that toads routinely batten on (fire ants, spiders, etc.), they must have pretty strong stomachs, and it is very unlikely that such a drastic measure as vomiting is used very often.

TOAD THE HUNTED

(Weasels, Stoats, and Ferrets, together:)
"Down with Toad! Down with Toad!
Toad! Toad! Down with Toad!
Down with the popular, successful Toad!"

A.A. MILNE, *TOAD OF TOAD HALL*

Given the toad's apparent biological mandate to multiply and replenish the earth, the typical toad couple producing many thousands of fertilized eggs each year, it is perhaps fortunate that toad enemies are so numerous and toads so vulnerable. Otherwise, within a very short time the entire surface of the earth would be carpeted with toads.

Perhaps it was some temporary disaster to anuran enemies that led to the biblical "plague of frogs":

> And Jehovah spake unto Moses, Go in unto Pharoah, and say unto him, Thus saith Jehovah, Let my people go, that they may serve me. And if thou refuse to let them go, behold, I will smite all thy borders with frogs: and the river shall swarm with frogs, which shall go up and come into thy house, and into thy bedchamber, and upon thy bed, and into the house of thy servants, and upon thy people, and into thine ovens, and into thy kneading troughs: and the frogs shall come up both upon thee, and upon thy people, and upon all thy servants.
>
> Exodus 8:1–4

A well-known herpetologist has argued recently that this plague of frogs was probably a plague of toads. (In Old Testament Hebrew there is only one word for both frogs and toads.) Whereas frog tadpoles metamorphose sporadically and generally stay near the water as adults, it is very common for toadlets to mature and leave the water en masse, this being one of their defensive strategies (send everybody at once, and a few will make it past the predators and survive). "Moreover, toadlets in Egyptian food would have been a far more serious matter than frogs since common toads in Egypt are toxic while common frogs are not" [Wassersug: 66–67].

The trial by toads did succeed in bending the Pharaoh's will temporarily, but after the amphibian guests all suddenly expired and their bodies were heaped in piles, even though the land stank, the stubborn Pharaoh hardened his heart once more.

The list of anuran enemies, or, more specifically, toad enemies, is a long one, and depredation begins early. The new-laid eggs are subject to fungal infections. Though generally distasteful, both eggs and young tadpoles of some species are tidbits for some types of fish (the absence of fish might explain the popularity of temporary ponds as breeding sites), water insects or their larvae, and tadpoles or young adults of other amphibians. They may also be eaten by salamanders, turtles, and various wading birds.

Those that make it to metamorphosis enter a new world of peril. That awkward period of several hours when the flattened body and sprouted legs make it difficult to swim, and the not-yet-reabsorbed tail makes it impossible to hop with any speed, let alone grace, is just the period most favored by garter snakes looking for an easy meal [Wassersug: 66].

Thomas Eisner witnessed a further peril for young toadlets looking to begin life on land in the Arizona desert. Of thousands of tiny spadefoots, many seemed unable to get past the pond's muddy shoreline. A little digging revealed that they were being first sucked under and then sucked dry by horsefly larvae who had buried themselves jaws uppermost in the mud. In a grim, ironic reversal, flies (or at least their larvae) were eating toads. As Eisner and his colleagues note, "It is probable . . . that adult spadefoot toads might on occasion gulp down the very fly that as a larva digested one of the toad's childhood companions" [Greenberg: 293].

The smaller they are, the more vulnerable, but toads of all sizes are preyed upon by reptiles, birds, and mammals. It might be asked why, since most toads are toxic, they have so many enemies. The answer seems to be that for every species of toad that developed toxic potency, nature evolved several species of enemies who are either immune to the poison or have found a way of avoiding it. Thus, while many snakes will avoid toads altogether, a few species have made toads the mainstay of their diets. Hawks and owls have been found to eat toads, though there is some evidence that they much prefer common frogs, which suggests that they do not relish the toxin. Carrion crows and grey herons have been observed feeding on toads.

The fact is that except in the case of a few highly virulent toads, such as the giant toad *(Bufo marinus)* or the Colorado River toad *(Bufo alvarius),* the poison is often not a very effective defense. In the first place, it is a totally passive weapon; a toad, lacking teeth, fangs, or barbs, has no means of injecting poison into its enemy. Secondly, the glands that secrete the poison are localized in the skin, chiefly in a pair of large parotid (or parotoid) glands, usually visible as swellings adjacent to and somewhat behind the ear drums. The warts on a toad's back also produce poison, but most toads seem to secrete their venom only in response to physical pressure on the skin. Thus their best defense is usually activated only when they are already in direct contact with the enemy.

But many enemies have found ways to avoid the poison altogether. Sea gulls have learned to flip the toad over and eat everything but the dorsal skin. Raccoons have adopted a similar strategy with the Colorado River toad, whose poison has been known to kill large dogs who have only mouthed it for a moment: the raccoons will pull large adults right out of their breeding ponds, tear their bellies open and devour the insides, without ever contacting the poison glands [Grzimek: 429]. "Shorebirds have been observed ganging up on one toad, taking turns swallowing it—none able to keep it down—until the poison is eventually wiped off well enough so that one bird can hold it down without regurgitation" [Smith: 144]. The skunk is more efficient, tumbling the toad over and rubbing its back vigorously in the grass until the poison is both excreted and rubbed away, leaving a palatable dinner.

Other mammals, such as the European marten and possibly the

American badger, seem to be immune to toad poison and need take no special precautions. The Old World hedgehog not only seems to enjoy eating toads but has found a way to put the poison to its own use:

> Before dining, the animals chew on the toad's large, poison-bearing granular glands and take the toad venom into their mouths, where contact with mucous membranes creates frothing. With their tongues, the hedgehogs slather the froth on their spines, apparently as a protective device. Occasionally hedgehogs will rub an entire toad skin over their spines.
>
> [Love, 1981:16]

Even more bizarre are the depredations wrought upon adult common European, natterjack, and midwife toads by the *Lucilia* fly. Avoiding the lethal front end, this fly lays its eggs on a toad's back or sides. The larvae, hatching in a few days, crawl up into the toad's nose and penetrate to the brain. The dead body of the toad then becomes a *Lucilia* incubator and food supply [Grzimek: 369–370].

> *Edible, adj. good to eat, and wholesome to digest, as a worm to a toad, a toad to a snake, a snake to a pig, a pig to a man, and a man to a worm.*
>
> *Ambrose Bierce,* The Devil's Dictionary

Perhaps the most voracious toad-eaters are those varieties of snakes that are impervious to the poison; and certain it is that they strike terror into toad hearts. George Porter reports what happened when he introduced a hognose snake into a group of toads:

> Each toad immediately went into what, in humans, would be called hysterics, began to leap wildly about, and within a very few minutes all had turned a pale ghostlike beige in color, a perfect example of turning pale with fear.
>
> [G. Porter: 40]

Other observers have reported toads apparently impersonating possums, rolling over and playing dead when threatened by snakes—only it turned out they weren't playing, but had suffered some sort of temporary heart failure, and had literally passed out.

PENDANT IN THE FORM OF A
SNAKE CATCHING A FROG
Ebrié Peoples, Ivory Coast
gold alloy, 9.1 cm. x 3.3 cm.
19th century
The Brooklyn Museum
Frank L. Babbott Fund

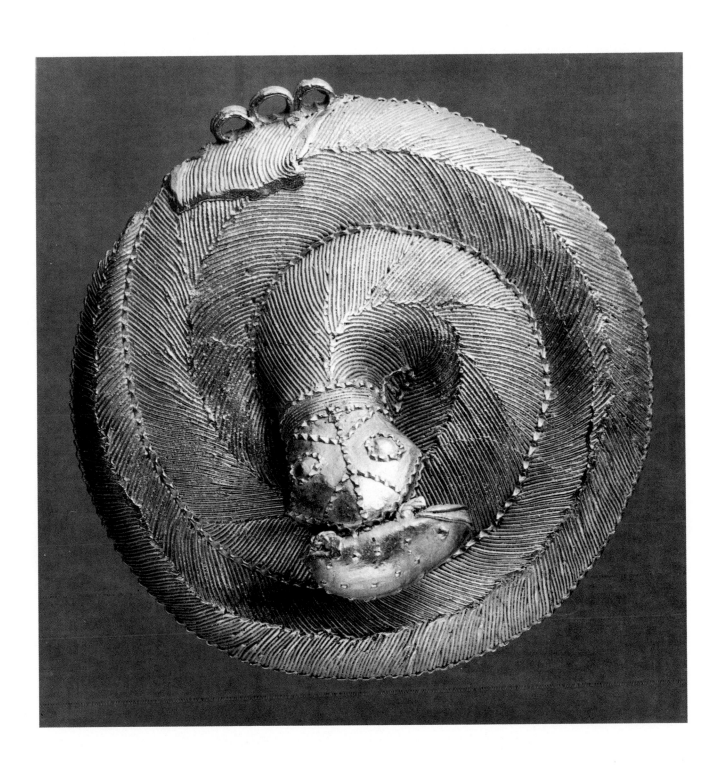

Toads who keep their heads do have a variety of less extreme defensive strategies. The simplest is to crouch motionless against the ground in order to escape observation. If detected, the toad may try to hop away or to sneak away, remaining in a crouched position and moving one leg at a time, very deliberately. If there is a large enough object nearby, the toad may try to hide behind it; or it may try to back into any nearby hole or crevice. If the soil is loose, it may try to dig itself under.

But if a toad-hungry snake is close, none of these strategies is likely to succeed. When actually confronted, the toad's last resort is to tuck its chin in and down facing the snake and to inflate its body with air. If the toad is large enough, relative to the snake, this additional body bulk may be enough to discourage a strike; or, if the toad is lucky enough to have backed into a crevice, the ballooning ploy may serve to wedge its body in place too firmly to be dislodged.

The fire-bellied toads of eastern Europe *(Bombina bombina* and *Bombina variegata)* puff themselves up in quite a different body position. These toads have bright red or yellow skin on the underside of their feet and bodies, which is quite thick and peppered with poison glands. When threatened, they confront the enemy with these shocking underparts, pumping toxic secretions at a great rate, while executing the "unken reflex"—a sort of hyperextended back arch in which both ends of the body curl up over the back while the belly remains on the ground [Bajger: 133].

Inflated in this position, the fire-bellied toad would seem to be about as invulnerable as any toad could be. But, alas, hungry grass snakes *(Natrix natrix)* have been known to get past even these defenses. As for the less toxic American *Bufo,* several animals can deal with his bloated condition. "Among them are snakes of the genus *Heterodon* which have enlarged, posterior, maxillary teeth that puncture the prey and release the air" [Bajger: 136].

Old Mr. Toad's Mistake

> If is a very little word to look at, but the biggest word you have
> ever seen doesn't begin to have so much meaning as little "if."
> If Jimmy Skunk hadn't ambled down the Crooked Little Path

just when he did; if he hadn't been looking for fat beetles; if he hadn't seen that big piece of bark at one side and decided to pull it over; if it hadn't been for all these "ifs," why, Old Mr. Toad wouldn't have made the mistake he did, and you wouldn't have had this story. But Jimmy Skunk did amble down the Crooked Little Path, he did look for beetles, and he did pull over that piece of bark. And when he pulled it over, he found Old Mr. Toad there.

Old Mr. Toad had crept under that piece of bark because he wanted to take a nap. But when Jimmy Skunk told him that he had seen Mr. Blacksnake that very morning, and that Mr. Blacksnake had asked after Old Mr. Toad, the very last bit of sleepiness left Old Mr. Toad. Yes, Sir, he was wide awake right away. You see, he knew right away why Mr. Blacksnake had asked after him. He knew that Mr. Blacksnake had a fondness for Toads. He turned quite pale when he heard that Mr. Blacksnake had asked after him, and right then he made his mistake. He was in such a hurry to get away from that neighborhood that he forgot to ask Jimmy Skunk just where he had seen Mr. Blacksnake. He hardly waited long enough to say good-bye to Jimmy Skunk, but started off as fast as he could go.

Now it just happened that Old Mr. Toad started up the Crooked Little Path, and it just happened that Mr. Blacksnake was coming down the Crooked Little Path. Now when people are very much afraid, they almost always seem to think that danger is behind instead of in front of them. It was so with Old Mr. Toad. Instead of watching out in front as he hopped along, he kept watching over his shoulder, and that was his second mistake. He was so sure that Mr. Blacksnake was somewhere behind him that he didn't look to see where he was going, and you know that people who don't look to see where they are going are almost sure to go headfirst right into trouble.

Old Mr. Toad went hopping up the Crooked Little Path as fast as he could, which wasn't very fast because he never can hop very fast. And all the time he kept looking behind for Mr. Blacksnake. Presently he came to a turn in the Crooked Little Path, and as he hurried around it, he almost ran into Mr. Blacksnake himself. It was a question which was more surprised. For just a wee second they stared at each other. Then Mr. Blacksnake's eyes began to sparkle.

"Good morning, Mr. Toad. Isn't this a beautiful morning? I was just thinking about you," said he.

But poor Old Mr. Toad didn't say good morning. He didn't say anything. He couldn't, because he was too scared. He just gave a frightened little squeal, turned around, and started down the Crooked Little Path twice as fast as he had come up. Mr. Blacksnake grinned and started after him, not very fast because he knew that he wouldn't have to run very fast to catch Old Mr. Toad, and he thought the exercise would do him good.

And this is how it happened that summer morning that jolly, bright Mr. Sun, looking down from the blue, blue sky and smiling to see how happy everybody seemed, suddenly discovered that there was one of the little meadow people who wasn't happy, but instead was terribly, terribly unhappy. It was Old Mr. Toad hopping down the Crooked Little Path for his life, while after him, and getting nearer and nearer, glided Mr. Blacksnake.

Thornton Burgess, *The Adventures of Old Mr. Toad*

Toads without friendly skunks to rescue them (such as the one who appears in Burgess's next chapter) would almost certainly be attacked under these conditions and pushed to their final defenses. The shrill scream of a seized toad might startle some predators into dropping their preys, but seems unlikely to affect a snake. Marchisin and Anderson suggest that the scream might "serve to attract animals that prey upon snakes," [154] but from a toad's point of view this seems a very long shot indeed. Face kicking, which they define as "pushing the predator's face with the hind legs when the prey is grasped by the head," seems a far more practical measure, and one which was observed to work in one instance by preventing the snake "from moving its jaws forward over the prey." The last desperate measure observed by these experimenters was the forceful expulsion of feces, which, as they aptly hypothesize, "may startle a predator as well as being distasteful" [Marchisin and Anderson: 152, 154].

One species of toad, as observed and recorded by R. Howard Hunt, has found an effective ally against its deadly enemy:

A western ribbon snake, its forked tongue flicking, slipped

through boulder-strewn prairie grass hunting for prey. Abruptly, it paused at a limestone slab and began to flick its tongue more rapidly, sampling the air for the chemical cues that would tell it a toad was near. Nearby, a narrow-mouthed toad dipped and darted about a small hole from which a ceaseless stream of ants flowed. Its attention was riveted upon the hole and the delectable ants. Suddenly, a striped blur hit the nickel-sized toad, engulfing it almost instantly. As the ribbon snake's jaws enveloped the toad's entire body, the doomed animal kicked and struggled, but the quivering bulge moved farther and farther down until it was only a muscular ripple carrying the small morsel to the snake's stomach.

Undetected by the ribbon snake, a second narrow-mouthed toad hunched hard against one flat edge of the limestone slab. The toad had seen the approaching snake and had stopped dead still, its pointed snout pressed into the soil. But the sham did not work, for the snake again slithered forward toward the small, brown lump that was the toad. The lump stirred, then bounded to the only escape possible—a burrow beneath the slab.

Sensing another meal, the ribbon snake followed the toad's scent trail, which led to the entrance to the burrow. And just beyond, at the edge of darkness, crouched the toad. With lidless eyes fixed on its prey, the snake tensed for a lunge. Suddenly a great hairy body, propelled by eight hairy legs, burst from the depths of the burrow, and a fully mature, female tarantula scuttled to within an inch of the toad. Taking advantage of the situation, the toad fled to safety—beneath the imposing black fangs of the tarantula. The confused snake reversed itself and disappeared into the waving grass. Danger past, the narrow-mouthed toad *Gastrophryne olivacea* wriggled from under its burrow companion, the giant tarantula, *Dugesiella hentzi*. [Hunt: 49]

The toads, several of whom may share a single tarantula burrow, repay this protection by devouring the numerous termites and fire ants that the burrow attracts, and which would be a great nuisance to the spider. Nor do the grateful toads ever ingest the spider's young, though perhaps this is because the infant spiders are protected by many painfully barbed hairs [Hunt: 52–53].

Apart from unique protective arrangements of this sort, the safest toads are undoubtedly the largest individuals of the largest-sized species, having the most virulent poison. Such is the giant (or marine) toad, *Bufo marinus*—indeed a formidable customer. It may be up to ten inches long, and secretes one of the most potent poisons in the natural world. Because of its eating abilities—it is capable of devouring half its body weight in insects and/or small reptiles and rodents at a sitting—it has been exported from its home in South and Central America to many other tropical or semitropical regions around the world, especially where sugar cane requires protection from sugar cane beetles. But its presence has not always been regarded as an unmixed blessing.

In 1967, Leonard Licht reported an incident in Peru in which giant-toad eggs were apparently boiled in water and made into a breakfast soup by a young Indian family:

> About 10 A.M. all four members of the family began to vomit . . . The mother and sister were prostrate, and their lips and fingers were blue; pustules had formed on [the] sister's lips. The abdomens of both the mother and sister appeared bloated and their bodies were hot and quite rigid. They were pronounced dead by 12 noon . . . The Peruvian intern in charge believed death was due to "cardiac seizure" preceded by respiratory difficulties.
>
> [Licht, 1967: 141]

A brother and older sister, who had eaten very little of the soup, recovered after bouts of fever, respiratory difficulties, and irregular heartbeat.

The presence of these "deadly toads"—whose very eggs could be lethal—in and around Miami and throughout heavily populated southeast Florida was greeted by *Science News* in 1967 as "a plague." For one thing, the toads' "cobra-like venom" was sending an endless procession of stricken pets to veterinary offices, many of them never to recover. Even more distressing were a few incidents involving humans. One man ran over a giant toad with his power mower and received a spray of poison in the face: "within minutes, the man's lips and cheeks were painfully swollen and it was days before he recovered" [Gebhart: 39]. In another incident, a Miami housewife was awakened one morning by the barking of her two dogs, and rose to find that her young

terrier had bitten a giant toad and was foaming at the mouth. She got a rag and was attempting to wipe away the foam when she very slightly scratched her right thumb on one of the dog's teeth; the reaction was almost incredible. Even though only the tiniest amount of venom could have entered her body, and that diluted by the dog's saliva, the woman reported almost instant nausea, and within minutes her right hand was swollen and the entire arm felt paralyzed. She required four weeks for full recovery; the terrier was dead in an hour and a half [Gebhart: 38–39].

Giant Toad

I am too big, too big by far. Pity me.

My eyes bulge and hurt. They are my one great beauty, even so. They see too much, above, below, and yet there is not much to see. The rain has stopped. The mist is gathering on my skin in drops. The drops run down my back, run from

BUFO MARINUS
Terence Shortt
watercolor on paper
29.5 x 37.0 cm., 1946
Collection of Martina R. Norelli
Photo by Gene Young

the corners of my down-turned mouth, run down my sides and drip beneath my belly. Perhaps the droplets on my mottled hide are pretty, like dewdrops, silver on a moldering leaf? They chill me through and through. I feel my colors changing now, my pigments gradually shudder and shift over.

Now I shall get beneath that overhanging ledge. Slowly. Hop. Two or three times more, silently. That was too far. I'm standing up. The lichen's gray, and rough to my front feet. Get down. Turn facing out, it's safer. Don't breathe until the snail gets by. But we go travelling the same weathers.

Swallow the air and mouthfuls of cold mist. Give voice, just once. O how it echoed from the rock! What a profound, angelic bell I rang!

I live, I breathe, by swallowing. Once, some naughty children picked me up, me and two brothers. They set us down again somewhere and in our mouths they put lit cigarettes. We could not help but smoke them, to the end. I thought it was the death of me, but when I was entirely filled with smoke, when my slack mouth was burning, and all my tripes were hot and dry, they let us go. But I was sick for days.

I have big shoulders, like a boxer. They are not muscle, however, and their color is dark. They are my sacs of poison, the almost unused poison that I bear, my burden and my great responsibility. Big wings of poison, folded on my back. Beware, I am an angel in disguise; my wings are evil, but not deadly. If I will it, the poison could break through, blue-black, and dangerous to all. Blue-black fumes would rise upon the air. Beware, you frivolous crab.

Elizabeth Bishop

PART 2:
TOAD-HUMAN RELATIONS

THE PHARMACEUTICAL TOAD

Experience has proved the toad to be endowed with valuable qualities. If you run a stick through three toads, and, after having dried them in the sun, apply them to any pestilent tumor, they draw out all the poison, and the malady will disappear.

MARTIN LUTHER, *TABLE-TALK*

Martin Luther's toad recipe, from sixteenth-century Germany, is typical of the dozens of medical uses and abuses of the toad throughout history. Something about this ugly and vulnerable little creature seems to have rendered it irresistible to medicos, who over the centuries have staked some wonderfully wild claims for its healing powers.

Recently the toad has been described as "a 'veritable chemical factory,' containing hallucinogens, powerful anesthetics and chemicals that affect the heart and nervous system" [cited in Wallis: 60].

> The biochemistry of these [toad] secretions has now been investigated in detail and it is known that at least four distinct classes of biologically active substances are present in the sticky white secretions. These are:
> (1) biogenic amines, including adrenalin and dopamine;
> (2) alkaloids, including serotonin, bufotenine, and bufotenidine;

(3) steroids (bufogenins); and
(4) steroid esters, the bufotoxins.

[Beebee: 44]

It is little wonder, then, that *Bufo,* as a species of moveable drugstore, pops up in the materia medica or folk medicine of many human cultures, ancient and modern. And no doubt, in view of the fact that each toad species appears to have its own unique secretion, and in view of the bewildering variety of prescriptions calling for toad parts, it will take modern science some time yet to evaluate traditional toad recipes.

The most obvious chemical use of *Bufo*—to poison somebody—was recognized early in the Greco-Roman-Arabian tradition. According to Leeser (whose extensive research on the medical use of toads appeared only in a little-known medical journal in 1959), Dioscorides sums up classical opinion on the toad thus:

> It stirs up tumours; pallor vehemently deprives the body of colour so that it looks like boxwood; difficult breathing torments, and a heavy breath (foetor) from the mouth, singultus, and sometimes spontaneous seminal emission follows . . . (The patients) should be induced to walk and run vehemently because of the torpor which seizes them.

[Cited in Leeser: 176]

To this list of evils, Avicenna adds the following:

> inflammation, sometimes dryness of the fauces and throat; also turbidity of the eyes, vertigo, convulsions, dysentery, loathing, vomiting, mental decline, delirium, amentia (intellectual deterioration), and [toothlessness] . . .

[Cited in Leeser: 176]

As we have already seen, the ultimate effect of ingesting toad poison is death—a fact that is well known by the various Indian tribes of South America who have traditionally tipped their blowdarts with anuran extracts. Pagenstecher describes the way of the Choco Indians with the spadefoot toad as follows:

> The animal is placed in a tube of bamboo, the hands of the

operator being protected with leaves, and when some of the poison is desired the tube containing the toad is suspended high over a fire. The toad soon becomes covered with a yellow juice which is allowed to drop into bowls from which it is transferred to small pots in which it gradually acquires the consistence of curari. A further supply of the poison may later be obtained from the toads thus treated. The poison is smeared on to the tips of arrows which are shot into game from blowing tubes. A small stag is killed by a poisoned arrow in from two to four minutes, a jaguar in from four to eight minutes.   [Cited in Abel and Macht: 1532]

Malay criminals favor both the parotid secretions, "toad's milk," and toad bile as ingredients in various preparations (which might also include tree saps, snake bile, ash-pumpkin flowers, and mercury) to be applied to the skin of a victim or smeared upon his sleeping mat. If this fails to kill, at the very least it should result in an incurable skin disease. Toad bile is more reliably lethal when mixed with such items as the poison of spiny fishes and a small shot of powdered glass, to be hidden in a victim's food [Gimlette and Thomson: 105, 83].

Juvenal... described the skill of Roman women in murdering their husbands with various agents, one of which was toads' lungs. In the beginning of the fourteenth century, Bishop Guichard of Troyes was accused of poisoning the wife of Philippe le Bel with a preparation of scorpions, toads and spiders. During the sixteenth century, processes of extracting the toads' poison with salt were devised by murderers, especially the Italian poisoners. It was stated that the victims who took the salt succumbed quickly . . . In the beginning of the eighteenth century, toad poison was added to explosive shells. It was probably assumed that the enemy's death would be doubly assured if explosives were reenforced with poisons.
                                    [Chen and Jensen: 244]

In his *Life of Nash*, Oliver Goldsmith details a crisis point in the history of Bath, when a certain mean-spirited physician "conceived a design of ruining the city, by writing against the efficacy of the waters."

It was from a resentment of some affronts he had received there that he took this resolution; and accordingly published a pamphlet, by which he said, *he would cast a toad into the spring.*

In this situation of things it was that Nash first came into that city; and hearing the threat of this physician, he humorously assured the people that, if they would give him leave, he would charm away the poison of the Doctor's toad, as they usually charmed the venom of the tarantula, by music. He therefore was immediately enpowered to set up the force of a band of music against the poison of the Doctor's reptile. The company very sensibly increased; Nash triumphed, and the sovereignty of the city was decreed to him by every rank of people.   [ed. Cunningham, VII, 65]

Less susceptible to the charms of music are the effects of virulent toad poison taken internally, as in the several recorded cases of people who have committed involuntary suicide by mistaking poisonous toads for edible frogs [Boys and Smith: 8]. Apparently the toads contain two types of substances that can act in quite different ways upon the heart. A first crisis occurs in the body of the toad-eater when epinephrine-like substances are absorbed by the membranes of the mouth and throat; "they may speed the heart rate so much that an uncontrolled and lethal flutter results" [Smith: 144]. If the victim survives, these substances are quickly destroyed in the digestive tract. But now, absorbed through the stomach, digitalis-like substances are activated that may slow the heartbeat to a dead stop [Smith: 144].

But the pharmaceutical toad is more than an occasional agent of murder or accidental death. Leeser cites an old story from Forestus:

> A woman in Rome wanted to get rid of her hydropic husband and, meaning to poison him, gave him powdered toad; but, lo and behold, the man was cured from his hydropsy [edema] within a short time.   [Leeser: 177]

The Chinese seem to have been aware of the medical possibilities of toad venom, *ch'an su*, for hundreds of years, and to have used its digitalis-like properties in treating heart ailments, among other things. Pellets of dried toad-venom may still be bought today from Chinese druggists, who prescribe it for external "treatment of canker sores, sinusitis, and many local inflammatory conditions, in the relief of toothache, and in the arrest of hemorrhages from the gums" [Chen and Jensen: 245].

In the early medicine of many cultures the toad was commonly used to treat edema and tumors, perhaps because of the homeopathic implications of its habit of swelling itself up when threatened. Thus Leeser reports the following curious case from Proteoca:

> A man aged sixty, suffering from ascites and anasarca [varieties of edema], and who had used everything for it in vain, had on someone's advice 36 toads laid upon his abdomen through 12 hours, changing them from time to time; he then applied a forceful massage from the extremities to the trunk. After the first very restless night a copious evacuation of stools and urine followed. Within three days he felt great relief, so that he pursued this treatment with confidence, and was cured after a few days. The toads caused him a tremendous itching and shuddering, and particularly when they moved, general trembling, horripilation [erection of hair; goose flesh], spasmodic contractions of the abdominal muscles and clonic convulsions of the whole body, as from electric shocks, occurred alternately.   [Lesser: 177]

British medicine of the sixteenth and seventeenth centuries also gave much credit to powdered toad or toad ashes, as in William Salmon's *London Dispensatory* of 1702, which stated that "the poudre of a dry'd toad taken 5ss at a time or more, cures almost incurable dropsies [edema], carrying away the water by urine" [cited in Abel and Macht: 1532]. Similarly, a German medical professor of the seventeenth century, one Michael Etmüller, gives the following toad prescription:

> Transfixed (alive) in the month of July, dried, powdered (the head and entrails being removed) and administered in doses of twelve grains on alternate days, they furnish an excellent cure for dropsy.   [Cited in Abel and Macht: 1532]

Van Helmont, summarizing seventeenth-century tradition, notes that "authors aver that hydropsy is removed by increased excretion of urine if one ties two living toads to the kidney region" [cited in Leeser: 177]. Oddly enough, William Salmon concludes his discussion of the toad in *The New London Dispensatory* with what might be considered a "counter-diuretic" recipe: "The Ashes hung about the neck (as an amulet) cures pissing a bed, or the not holding of the Water" [Salmon: 201]. It's hard to see how one can have it both ways.

Early medical tradition as a whole seems to emphasize the diuretic use of toads, finding it a remedy not only for general swellings of the body, but also for more specific tumors. Thus Hahnemann, in 1795, notes:

> Externally the entire dried toads have been applied to the bubonic glands in plague, and pains and inflammation were alleged to have been relieved. Living eviscerated toads have been tied upon indurated glands and kept there for nine days, and the tumours are said to have been dissolved thereby. The powder of a burnt toad sprinkled into breast cancer is said to have been of benefit . . . Oil in which toads were boiled, too, was reputed to have removed glandular tumours and pains.
> [Cited in Leeser: 177]

Leeser traces the use of toads against bubonic plague back to the sixteenth century, when Paracelsus wrote:

> As to the other kind of plague which collects itself into a centrum (bubo), one should take toads well dried in the sun or in the air and put them straight on to the tumour. Then the toad swells up and attracts the plague poison through its whole skin, it grows large and full, and if it has filled up thus, it should be discarded and a fresh one should be put on . . . For thus evil takes away evil.   [Cited in Leeser: 177–178]

By the middle of the nineteenth century, Hencke of Riga was experimenting with *Bufo* in treating cancer:

> Hencke reported on three other cases of mammary cancer treated with *Bufo;* in two of them the primary tumour and the enlarged axillary glands disappeared, whereas for the third case it is merely stated that the shooting, lancinating pains disappeared almost immediately after a minute dose of *Bufo*.
> [Cited in Leeser: 182]

ILLUSTRATION FROM HORTUS
SANITATIS
1491
Chapin Library, Williams College

Leeser also traces the use of tincture of toad in the treatment of epilepsy beginning in mid-nineteenth-century France, and cites several cases of apparent cures. But case studies in the treatment of epilepsy, like those in the case of cancer, are fragmentary and usually either inconclusive or so embellished with folkloric detail as to be suspect. Nevertheless, from the effect of *Bufo* venom on the emotional and sexual impulses, Leeser deduces its focus in the ganglia of the brain stem and suggests the possibility of therapeutic effects for certain types of epilepsy [Leeser: 185].

Apparently there is some legitimate medical basis for other toad prescriptions as well. Abel and Macht were able to isolate bufagin, a digitalis-like substance from toad skin that would in fact be chemically effective in treating edema [Abel and Macht: 1535]. Read points out that "cinobufagin," like other members of the digitalis group, has a characteristic emetic effect [Read: 154]. Chen's work with the Chinese toad pill *ch'an su* indicates that its use "for hemorrhage of the gums and sinusitus appears justified because of the presence of adrenaline. Its anesthetic action accounts for its use for toothache and canker sores" [cited in Read: 154]. The presence of serotonin may also explain its power to stop bleeding [Leeser: 179].

Still, it is a bit difficult to believe in all the claims of materia medica. Will the flesh of the Indian toad *Bufo melanosticus* really cure gonorrhea, tuberculosis, and leprosy [Nadkarni: 217]? Is it a good idea to feed dried Asiatic toad venom, even when collected on the fifth day of the fifth moon, to one's infant by way of treating malnutrition [Read: 152]? What about toad grease for those rheumatic pains [Brandon: 218]? Will toad brain actually cure night blindness and clarify the vision [Read: 157]? And will "the foot of a great living toad being cut off when the moon is void of course, and hastens to the conjunction of the sun, [cure] one of the King's evil, being hung about their neck" [cited in Budge: I, 87]? Evidently modern science still has much to do in sorting out fact from fiction—that is, in locating and preserving the valid medical knowledge that is often buried under the kind of folklore illustrated by the following tale:

> According to the *Yi Shuo* by *Chang Kao* in the record of the *Che Ch'ing Tsa Shuo*, there was a man suffering from a wound on his foot which in winter was suddenly well till in the summer it suppurated and stunk, and was unspeakably painful. He met a Taoist who explained that because the man had walked through the grass he had annoyed some copulating snakes from which the semen had got into the wound and formed a baby snake, which rested inside in winter but came to life in the summer. He told the man to apply a mashed live toad three times a day. After the third day a small snake came out from the center of the wound, he removed it with iron pincers and then he got well. [Read: 157]

One early recipe—rather cosmetic than medical—that I see no cause to doubt is a sort of ancient "Chinese formula" hair dye:

> In the *Kou Lou Shen Shu* it says, collect a gill of tadpoles on the third day of the third month, dry them in the shade. Wait till the mulberries are ripe and then macerate the dried tadpoles in one pint of mulberry juice. Then bury the container below the east wall of the house for 100 days, after which the mixture turns into a kind of varnish. Applied to the whiskers and hair they will never become white again.
>
> [Cited in Read: 161]

At the other end of the toad medical-potency scale is the story related by M. F. K. Fisher in *A Cordiall Water*, of a superannuated Algerian woman who claimed to have been brought back from the dead by her mother's application of fresh pigeon's blood to her head and a pillowcaseful of live toads ("all hopping and thumping in the bottom of the funeral bed") to her feet. "Am I not right," the old woman concludes, "to call the toad my friend?" [Fisher: 49–50]

No doubt she is, but the zombies of Haiti have far less reason to be grateful to the toad. According to a 1983 report in *Time* [Wallis: 60], the Harvard botanist E. Wade Davis discovered that the potion that victims are forced to drink is a coma-inducing concoction of *Bufo marinus* and toxic puffer fish. When they are properly dosed, the incipient zombies' trance is so deep that it appears to be death itself. Next they are buried, only to be exhumed by the voodoo chiefs (within about eight hours or so, to avoid asphyxiation), fed a paste of the potently hallucinogenic "zombie cucumber," and led away to work as slaves on sugar plantations. Ironically, the effects on the central nervous system are such that they fail to make very good workers. As Desterne discovered way back in 1859 and 1860, by feeding his subjects extracts of toad skin in alcohol, the psychic effects included "depression and extreme irritability, *irritable, impatient temper, irascible, little inclination to work*" [cited in Leeser: 183].

Perhaps inspired by the toad's illustrious medical history, Felix Mann, in 1959, published "The Homeopathic Toad," a hilarious tongue-in-cheek misapplication of homeopathic principles to the matching of patient and therapy. A portion of that essay follows:

> In broad terms: a person who looks like a toad is a candidate for *Bufo* therapy. A person who looks like the human organic counterpart of the toad, namely the colon, is also a candidate for *Bufo* therapy . . . .
>
> If I might be allowed to exaggerate a little, I would say that a toad is nothing but a human colon; those forces which in the human are concentrated in the colon are in the animal kingdom concentrated in the toad. It might be said that from the point of view of living forces the whole toad has become a colon; the animal is bubbling over with colonic forces so that the whole of it has become transformed into a large intestine.

There are three types of *Bufo* patients:

(1) The constitutional type.

He was born to look like a toad. When he is healthy and full of life he looks like a toad; his wisdom comes from the depths of his belly. He looks just healthy and at home the way he looks. When he loses his toad-like expression he is ill.

Bufo medication should not be used in this type of patient.

(2) The patient with a deficiency of *Bufo* force.

He has lost this force that springs out from the depths of his belly. His colon and the rest of his body which are normally permeated with this force are now dead and are either hypoactive or function in an autonomous manner without being permeated by the function of other parts of the body. This type looks like a dead toad, like an ashen colon, which has already burnt the fire of its life.

This type of patient is ideal for *Bufo* therapy.

(3) The patient with an excess of *Bufo* force.

He bubbles over with an excess of *Bufo* force. It permeates his whole body, his whole body begins to look like a seething hot colon. He turns into a toad.

BUFOTENINE, SHAMANISM, & TOAD THE EARTH MOTHER

O ne of the more intriguing components of toad secretions is bufotenine, a poisonous hallucinogenic alkaloid (5-hydroxy-N, N-dimethyltryptamine) first isolated from the skin glands of the common toad and since discovered in various plants. Actually, there is some question as to how readily unmodified bufotenine can penetrate the blood-brain barrier to produce hallucination. But the family of potent hallucinogenic alkaloids to which it belongs, mostly derivable from mushrooms and other plants, seems to have been used by humans all the way back to Neanderthal man one hundred thousand years ago—and perhaps even earlier [Furst, 1972a: xvii, ix].

Some modern theorists have suggested that early shamanic cultures —such as that of prehistoric Siberia, based on the fly agaric mush-room—represent the beginning of religion. Shamanism may be the Ur-religion, dating back to the Stone Age and eventually giving rise to all the world's religions [Furst, 1972a: viii–ix]. It seems to have spread from northern Asia into India and Europe, and over the Bering land-bridge into the New World, where it is still widely practiced in Central and South America.

At the heart of the shamanic culture is the shaman, whose essential role is that of mediator between his people and the spirit world. By his influence over good and evil spirits he can prevent or inflict disease and death; predict events; control the weather, the supply of game animals, and the success of the hunt; and curry the goodwill of his tribe's deities. And his ticket to the spirit world is often, though not always, a particular hallucinogenic plant.

The toad is important in shamanic societies in two major ways. Physically, whole toads or parts of toads were apparently added to the hallucinogenic brew in certain ancient shamanic cultures, perhaps for added potency or tang. Presumably some other ingredient, or some feature of the preparation process, served to neutralize its toxicity.

More pervasively, the toad seems to be part of the symbolic or mythological side of the shamanic ritual. For one thing, the toad is often associated with the psychedelic mushroom (originally "toad stool"), not only in European tradition [Wasson: 185–194] but also in the New World. Mayan excavation sites in highland Guatemala, for example, have yielded numerous "mushroom stones" dating from about 500 B.C. One of these now in the collection of the National Museum of Guatemala shows a mushroom growing out of a crouching toad with a humanized face [Schultes: 58]. In fact, the toad figure in various guises, often with overlaid human or jaguar features, is very common in the arts of the pre-Columbian New World.

A solid body of toad mythology lies behind this prominence of the toad in Meso-American art. At its center, according to the American ethnologist Peter T. Furst, is the recurring figure of the toad as Earth Mother, the giver and taker of life. In the Aztec art of central Mexico, for instance,

> she is depicted sometimes as a real toad, more commonly as a clawed, anthropomorphic being in the characteristic up-right squatting position in which women in the traditional world customarily give birth. Her joints are adorned with human skulls, her fanged mouth is the maw of the Netherworld through which the human dead and dying sun pass into her transforming womb in a never-ending cycle of destruction and rebirth.   [Furst, 1976: 158]

This creature, Tlaltecuhtli, became the literal source of creation, when Quetzalcoatl the bird serpent and Tezcatlipoca the magician-jaguar found her "floating alone in the primordial seas" and tore her body in half—one half then forming the heavens, the other half the earth. In return for bringing forth edible plants out of her body, she receives the bodies of humans at their burial, thus becoming both the source and the end of life. Furst suggests that the toad's impressive fertility on one hand and its cannibalism of its own or related species on the other made it right for the part; furthermore, its literal metamorphosis from water to land animal and its role in serving the shaman's transcendence from the physical to the spiritual world incorporate the basic Amerindian principle of transformation [Furst, 1976: 159].

This recognition of the symbolic importance of the toad has enabled Furst [1981] and other scholars to come up with some interesting hypotheses about the artworks of native American civilizations, especially the Olmec of southern Mexico and Central America. One common figure in the stone carvings of this oldest American culture (which began about 1000 B.C.) is the so-called "were-jaguar," usually described as a composite of jaguar features and those of a human baby. But Furst points out that though features of jaguars and birds may be incorporated in the figure, its primary form is often that of a toad with a gaping, toothless mouth. Its most important symbolic features are the triangular cleft in the forehead and what were formerly considered jaguar fangs at the corners of its mouth. The V-shaped cleft may suggest the deep furrow in the heads of some male jaguars [Bernal: 72–73; cited in Furst, 1981: 150], it is even more clearly seen in a frontal view of the heads of toads local to tropical lowland Mexico, *Bufo marinus* and *Bufo valliceps*. (Skeletal remains of these toads have been found at Olmec and Mayan burial sites.) The V-cleft, a feature also shared by crocodilians, is a universal symbol for the female reproductive anatomy, reinforcing what seems to be another widespread connection—that of the toad with female fertility. And, as Furst demonstrates, in Mesoamerican art it can function "as a kind of cosmic vaginal passage through which plants or ancestors emerge from the underworld" [Furst, 1981:151].

Furst's interpretation of the "jaguar fangs" is also appropriate to the toad as earth mother. He suggests that they are not really fangs at all; indeed, they do not look like fangs, but scholars who knew the jaguar's

importance for the Olmec assumed that that was what they must be. Furst proposes instead that the curling tails trailing from the toothless toad mouth in Olmec art actually represent the last vestiges of old skin being swallowed by *Bufo marinus* in its moulting process. As the toad swallows its old skin, which splits along the spinal column and up the belly and is loosened by repeated swellings and shrinkings of the toad's body, then pulled off in a symmetrical pattern as it is being eaten, the skin of the hind legs reproduces the V-cleft, while that of the front body and legs (the last to be swallowed) dangles in bands from the corners of the mouth. Thus the toad is periodically reborn by consuming itself, symbolizing

the drama of cyclical death and rebirth in the earth. By depicting in a composite image this extraordinary process in the toad as the earth's metaphor precisely at the point when

GIANT TOAD SWALLOWING
ITS SKIN *(above)*
Photo by Peter T. Furst

EFFIGY JAR IN FORM OF
FROG *(right)*
pottery, h. 17.2cm., w. 15.2 cm.
Peru, North Coast, Mochica?
c. 500 A.D.
The Montreal Museum of
Fine Arts
Gift of Hon. Emile Vaillancourt
Photo by Christine Guest, MMFA

the animal is altogether free of its dead epidermis, while the last of it is still being sucked into its own toothless mouth, the Olmec artist has admirably succeeded in synthesizing destruction and regeneration in a single image.

[Furst, 1981:160]

Furst's hypothesis is supported by the fact that the humped position of the moulting toad is the precise position of the toad figures etched or sculpted in basalt slabs (altars?) at several Central American sites [Furst, 1981:159].

The toad's earth-mother connection with the underworld may serve to explain the presence of actual toad bones as well as carved jade

toad figures, toad ax heads, and toad effigy bowls at various Olmec and Mayan burial sites. There is also the possibility that these objects were used in some ritual—that the toad effigy jars, bowls, or pots were used in the preparation of a hallucinogenic brew by means of which the celebrants could themselves be transported to the spirit world.

Though not with such central importance, the toad figure appears in some way in the art, myth, or folklore of almost every culture from Mexico through Central America to northern South America, and from the Olmecs to the present day. Many of its associations are with rain and fertility. The toad/frog figure appears in Mayan art as the servant of the rain gods. Sometimes she is shown with maize growing out of her head.

As keeper of rains, agent of fertility, the toad may demand human sacrifice—the drenching of the earth with blood or tears. The mysterious ball-game rituals of Olmecs, Aztecs, and others, in which apparently the winners were sacrificed, is commemorated in many elaborately carved stone yokes, many of them portraying a stylized toad. An interesting postscript is the following: F. Depons, traveling in South

America during the years 1801 to 1804, found tribes of Indians along the Orinoco who turned the tables by holding the toads personally responsible for the weather, thus paying to them "the honours due to the divinity":

> Far from injuring these animals, they carefully kept them
> under pots, in order to obtain rain or fine weather; and so fully

MUMMY PONCHO
*cotton and wool, tabby and
tapestry weave with
felines and frogs
h. 67.3 cm., w. 26.6cm.
Peru, South Coast, Nasca
400 B.C.–300 A.D.
The Montreal Museum
of Fine Arts
D.W. Parker Fund
Photo by Marilyn Aitken, MMFA*

COSTA RICAN GOLD FROG
PENDANT
Ancient Art of the Andes
3.1 cm.
The Brooklyn Museum
Purchased from John Wise Ltd.
1934

persuaded were they of their power in this respect, that they
scourged them as often as their petitions were not answered.
[Cited in Roth: 138–39]

At least this expedient seems something of an advance over human
sacrifice.

Some of the most beautiful frog and toad artifacts were produced
by the Diquis culture of Costa Rica (1000–1550 A.D.) in the form of

elaborate gold pendants. Some of these have what appears to be a stylized version of the ancient Olmec toad skin attached to the mouth, complete with V-cleft. It is tempting to believe that these pendants were based directly upon the beautiful golden toad of Costa Rica *(Bufo periglenes),* now surviving only in a few square miles of the Monteverde Cloud Forest Reserve.

Earring Toad

There was a saying
Toad knew too much
He was too full of himself.
He was puffed up like a cloud.

Man bought him a one-way ticket
To the land of the stone,
The deaf stone, and the bog.
Woman, however, knew better,

Suspected something and followed.
"Tell me everything," she said,
But toad had his conditions.
Woman returned

With a hole in each ear,
And dangling from a gold wire
In each ear
Was a small golden toad.

Now man grows nervous
When woman stares off into space
Conversing, apparently,
With only herself.

Susan Fromberg Schaeffer

THE ORIENTAL TOAD

The eye a mirror
the mouth open
like a washbasin
you may be sure
the toad is a goblin.

This rendering of a Chinese poem, by Lafcadio Hearn, is reprinted by T. Volker [169], who points out that its final word in Chinese is a pun for "toilet-article." The pun suggests a complexity of tone that seems widespread in Asian toad myths and stories: on the one hand, the toad is respected as a creature of supernatural power; on the other, it is viewed with affectionate warmth and described with wit.

Probably the best known of the Chinese toad legends concerns one Liu Hai and his pet, the three-legged toad Ch'an Chu (sometimes called Hsia ma). Liu Hai was apparently a real person, a minister of the tenth century who gave up politics in favor of the ascetic life and the study of Taoist magic. It is reported that he eventually found the secret of immortality. In Chinese and Japanese traditions, magic is usually presided over by the toad, who is a Houdini-like master of the art of escape, can make pills that transform humans into toads (or vice versa), and knows the secret of eternal life. How Liu Hai first befriended Ch'an is not clear. According to one story he was employed to get rid of a toad

living in a deep pool, whose noxious vapors were polluting a whole neighborhood. He lured the toad within reach by dangling five gold coins on a string, and then destroyed it—thus illustrating the evils of avarice. Unaccountably, however, Ch'an reappears in centuries of Chinese scroll paintings as Liu Hai's friend and confidant. Occasionally tiring of transporting Liu around the globe, Ch'an may pop down the occasional well for a break, but he always permits himself to be lured back to work by those dangling coins.

The double figure of wise-teacher-and-toad-companion was imported by the Japanese as the *gama sennin,* a sort of toad-guru also known as Kosensei. An ugly man, his skin mottled with warts and pimples, he lived as a mountain hermit in the sole company of a giant toad, and supported himself by selling herbs with magical properties. His secrets had been taught him as a reward by his demon-toad familiar,

BIRTHDAY CELEBRATION BY
FOUR IMMORTALS *(above)*
Shang Hsi
Ming Dynasty (1368–1644)
National Palace Museum
Taipei, Taiwan
Republic of China

HSIA-MO *(right)*
ink and color on silk
105 x 38 cm.
14th century, Chinese
The Cleveland Museum of Art
Edward L. Whittemore Fund,
82.30

GAMA SENNIN, OR KOSENSEI (HOU HSIEN SHENG) AND HIS THREE-LEGGED TOAD
Soga Shohaku
paper kakemono, 109.1 x 42.2 cm.
Japan, Edo Period
(18th century), Soga school
Courtesy of the Freer Gallery
of Art, 04.192
Smithsonian Institution
Washington, D.C.

whom he had found sick and nursed back to health. As a matter of convenience, Ko could turn himself into a toad while bathing. He is commonly pictured sitting under, beside, or upon his toad, sometimes feeding it a longevity pill [Volker: 168].

Toad magic is not always this white in Far Eastern mythology. The legendary Japanese demon-toad O Gama of Suwo was a monster that ate snakes and could destroy a large area by spitting poison. Karu, the goddess of fever, is accompanied by a yellow toad riding on a fish [Volker: 168]. The *gama* as evil goblin could create wonderful illusions in the mist of its breath, luring insects, animals, or humans to their destruction [Jobes: 1582]. In fact, the ancient Japanese regarded the mysteriously wise and well-traveled toad as the fitting companion of the Woman of the Three Road River (a Japanese version of the Styx), and carved its figure upon the naked knee of Emma O, the Regent of Hell [Belt: 42].

Chinese dualistic philosophy is equally ill-disposed to the toad, who is lumped together with other loathsome creatures that represent the evil, dark feminine forces of *yin* (as opposed to the good, masculine forces of light, known collectively as *yang*). In art these negative forces are represented as the "five poisons"—the spider, lizard, centipede, snake, and toad—all equally and interchangeably detestable. Since it was thought that images of these animals could ward off the evils they represented, one or another of them is often shown in Chinese art being trodden underfoot by the spirit-tiger of the Taoist master Chang Tao-ling [Runes and Schrickel: 982]. This group of creatures seems to underlie another common configuration—a triangular standoff of snake, toad, and snail (or centipede). Since snake eats toad, toad eats snail, and the slime of the snail is said to destroy the snake, the point seems to be that evil negates itself.

Symbolically, the ultimate *yin* manifestation is the moon, so it is no surprise that the Chinese see not a man but a toad in the moon. According to legend, when Yao's throne was being taken over by Shun back in the third millennium B.C., ten suns appeared, threatening to scorch the earth. With a magic bow given him by Shun, the inimitable archer Shen I shot nine of the suns out of the sky. The Queen of the Western Paradise rewarded him with the pill of immortality and a permanent residence on the remaining sun (the ultimate *yang*). But

Shen I's wife, Ch'ang O, stole the pill, swallowed it, and made off to the moon to escape her husband's wrath. There she spit up the pill's outer covering, which turned into a white rabbit, and she herself was transformed into a three-legged toad.

> Despite her fickle misdeed, Shen I's love for Ch'ang O was such that he built her the Palace of the Great Cold on the moon decorated with precious stones and pillars of cinnamon. There he visits her on the fifteenth day of each month, a fact which accounts for the unusual brilliance of the moon at this time. [Belt: 40]

Thus in the Far East the creature that inhabits the moon is sometimes seen as a white hare, sometimes as a toad, though by the Han dynasty (200 B.C.) they are usually regarded as living there together.

THREE-LEGGED TOAD
jade 6.7 x 13 cm.
China, Qing Dynasty
18th century
The Montreal Museum of Fine Arts
Gift of Mrs. W. Hugh Owen
Photo by Christine Guest, MMFA

> A splendid Thang mirror shows one resolution of the problem, for on it the hare is already on the moon and preparing the elixir of immortality which Heng-o is to drink to become an immortal toad, shown near the foot of the cassia tree, which is also on the moon. [Christie: 63]

Apparently not satisfied with pills, occasionally this moon-toad attempts to swallow the moon itself, causing an eclipse; or perhaps its periodic swallowing is an agency of the moon's renewal and thus another way of symbolizing immortality. In some representations, immortality is indicated by a fungus growing out of the toad's forehead—*ling chih,* the fungus of immortality, normally a woody growth on tree trunks [Belt: 39]. In the several tomb murals of the Han period, as Michael Loewe notes,

MEDITATION
Clifton Karhu
woodblock print, 1970
Photo by Judith DeGraaff

the hare is shown pounding his drugs with his pestle and mortar; sometimes the toad dances with glee, holding a strange object in his hands; we may surmise that he is in a state of euphoria induced by taking a dose, and near to the state of immortality so greatly desired.   [Loewe: 54–55]

It remains only to suggest the interesting parallels between this pattern of oriental toad mythology and the toad-shamanism of the New World. Here perhaps Furst deserves the last word:

The use of *Bufo* poison as magical folk medicine in Mexico recalls Chinese Taoist and derivative Japanese traditions of the *Gama sennin*, a wise teacher and accomplished herbalist who lived alone in the mountains in the company of a giant toad. The toad, who in some versions is really the *Gama sennin* himself (*Gama* means "toad" in Japanese), taught him the magical and healing arts, including the making of pills that enabled him to transform at will into toad form. There are also Japanese and earlier Chinese traditions of toads capable of conjuring up the most exquisite visions, especially a vision that brought one face to face with the Taoist Islands of Paradise, in whose center stood a giant immortal pine amid the most beautiful flowers, trees, and animals that symbolized eternal life; among these is the fungus of immortality, the legendary Ling Chih, whose real ancestor may have been the fly agaric of Eurasiatic shamanism. What is more, the dwellers of this blessed island stayed eternally young by drinking from the fountain of life at the foot of the enormous, never decaying pine.   [Furst, 1976:162]

THE EVIL MEDIEVAL TOAD

Much of medieval Western zoology was based on the work of classical authors, but when it came to descriptions of the toad there wasn't much to go on. As I noted earlier, the ancient Egyptians may not have made a distinction between frogs and toads—at least, not before the second of the ten plagues. They did worship a goddess of childbirth, one Heket, who is usually pictured with a frog's head. They also crafted oil lamps and amulets in amphibian shapes. It is possible that the oil lamps were frogs, burning with Heket's light of life, and that the amulets (some of which are covered with a wart-like stippling) are meant to represent toads and were worn to ward off evil. Both lamps and amulets were sometimes buried with the dead, perhaps to repel the threatening demons of the underworld [Egger: 16–17].

The Greeks and Romans did distinguish between frogs and toads, but appear to have paid very little attention to either; at least amphibian figures almost never appear in their arts, crafts, myths, or literature. Early Greek culture knew a Phrygian god named Sabazius who was associated with the toad [Cooper: 174]; later Greeks identified him with Dionysus, the orgiastic god of wine and revelry [Parrinder: 238]. It is possible that Sabazius presided over an ancient toad-toadstool-shamanic cult like those of Eurasia and the New World, but too little is known to justify anything but speculation.

Most classical Western writers on the animal world, such as Aristotle and Aelian, do little more than list the toad as a poisonous land-dwelling counterpart to the frog. Virgil, in his *Georgics*, lumps the toad with moles, mice, ants, and weevils, as a noxious creature that plagues the earth. In Athens, the word for "toad" was used as a nickname for certain courtesans with bad complexions [Liddell and Scott: 1958]. Only the elder Pliny (*Natural History*, Book 32) goes into some detail, defining the toad as a frog who lives only in brambles, a "bramble-toad," and as large, horned, and full of poison. He also includes a few of the marvelous stories about toads that were to proliferate throughout the Middle Ages: that the presence of a toad will cause a meeting of people to fall silent; that a small bone in its right side will stop water from boiling; that a bone in its left side will repel the attacks of dogs, or, if worn as an amulet, will act as an aphrodisiac [Pliny: 495].

Such was the state of things when an anonymous author, working in or near Alexandria in about the fourth century, put together a small book of animal descriptions; his pen name, Physiologus, signifying "a natural historian," soon became the title of the work itself. In it he drew upon classical authors, biblical materials, travelers' tales, and folklore, to create a series of brief animal sketches whose purpose was to illustrate Christian truths. For him the realm of animal behavior was a happy hunting ground for fantastic analogies—the natural world a secret code to reveal divine mysteries to the initiated. Thus in his section 46, "On the Frog," he differentiates frogs "from the dry place" (which I take to mean land-dwelling, dry-skinned toads), which he claims are killed by summer rain, and frogs who live in bodies of water:

> "The ones from the dry place" represent fine, abstinent men who are unaffected by working patiently in abstinence; however, if they are caught in the rain (that is, in worldly desires), they die. The water frogs, however, are those who cannot stand abstinence. If these abstain until daytime, not

being able to bear a ray of intelligible sunlight, they slip back
again into their former desires.   [Curley: 60–61]

This small book enjoyed enormous popularity and became the matrix
of dozens of bestiaries for the next thousand years and more. The great
medieval flowering of unnatural history endowed many animals,
including the toad, with bizarre magical or alchemical qualities that
were based more on symbolism or arcane theories of sympathetic or
antipathetic properties than on zoology.

One Theophilus, for instance, gives directions for turning red
copper into Spanish gold by using powdered basilisk, human blood, and
vinegar. The first problem is to get hold of a basilisk; for this it is useful
to know some crafty Gentiles, who are skilled in the following process
of creating them:

> They have an underground chamber completely walled in on
> all sides with stone, and with two windows so small as scarcely
> to admit any light. In this they put two cocks of twelve or
> fifteen years and give them plenty of food. These, when they
> have grown fat, from the heat of their fat have commerce
> together and lay eggs. As soon as the eggs are laid the cocks
> are ejected and toads are put in to sit on the eggs and are fed
> upon bread. When the eggs are hatched chicks come forth
> who look like young roosters, but after seven days they grow
> serpents' tails and would straightway burrow into the ground,
> were the chamber not paved with stone.
> [Cited in Thorndike, 1: 771]

Once you've made it this far, the rest is easy. You bury the young
basilisks for six months in perforated brass pots with copper lids, then
roast and powder them, adding one third of the blood of a ruddy man
(also powdered). Tempered with vinegar, this forms just the right
mixture for smelting down the copper into gold.

Michael Scot, in his *De Alchemia*, also found alchemical virtues in
the toad. "As the first step in the preparation of a marvelous powder for
purposes of transmutation," he recommended that five toads be "shut
up in a vessel and made to drink the juices of various herbs with vinegar"
[Thorndike, 2: 337]. And as late as 1604, Guibert reports that the team

of Porta and Pizzimenti once succeeded in turning mercury into silver by heating it up with a toad in an earthenware pot over a slow fire. Before it was consumed, the drying toad absorbed a good deal of the mercury, converting it to silver, but, unfortunately, "they never could attain the same result again" [Thorndike, 6: 245].

In addition to its alchemical wizardry, the toad was credited in the Middle Ages with many other magical manifestations. Thomas of Cantimpre, for instance, records the punishment of an undutiful son who failed to support his aging father. It appears that a toad leapt into his face and attached itself too firmly to be removed. There it remained as a disfiguring tumor, prompting the resident bishop to send the unlucky young man on a circuit of the diocese, a walking moral warning against the sin of ingratitude [Thorndike, 2: 381].

Other writers have recorded even more intimate relations between the toad and the human body. Aldrovandi notes that

> in 1553, on a certain farm in Thuringia near Unstrum, a toad with a tail was born to a woman. . . . Nor is this surprising, since Coelius Aurelianus and Platearius write that women sometimes give birth, along with a human fetus, to toads and other animals of this kind.
>
> [Latin translation by George Frear]

Platearius suggests that menstrual aids induce these monstrous conceptions, and points out that women in Salerno drink a potent juice of celery and leeks at the first sign of pregnancy to destroy any uterine intruders. "Moreover a certain woman from Gesnerum, when as a recent bride she was said in the opinion of all to be pregnant, gave birth to four animals similar to toads and was in the best of health" [Frear translation; cited in Gubernatis: 383].

Topsell offers a more natural explanation for the occurrence of toads in men's stomachs. Although he claims that toads are sometimes spontaneously generated in the earth, he doubts that there is sufficient putrefaction in the human body to produce so intricate a creature— worms, yes, but not toads. What happens is that a man swallows a toad egg in his drinking water; the egg, being viscous, sticks to the wall of his stomach and there develops into a full-grown toad. Since its material

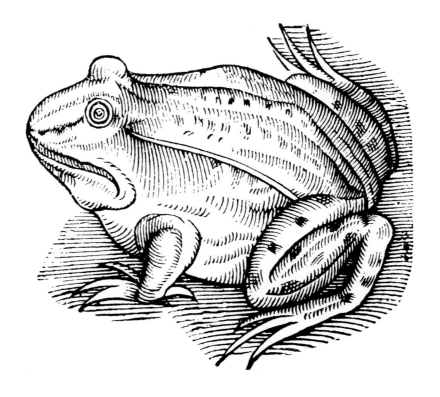

makeup is contrary to man's, it can be neither digested nor voided. The absence of air will not bother it; after all, a toad can live for years in the heart of a tree or a rock. Eventually, though, its venom will ripen and slowly poison its host unless a strong dose of snake fat is drunk, which will bring about spasms of vomiting violent enough to expel the toad [Topsell: 728]. Other medieval writers also cite cases of humans vomiting toads, though one, Lucas Schroeck, disagrees with Topsell in one minor point when he records the case of a toad being excreted [Thorndike, 8: 245].

Another likely place to find toads in the human body was in abscesses:

Paul de Sorbait saw with his own eyes a live toad issue from an abscess of a vintress who had contracted goitre by drinking cold and dirty water. Paul hazards the conjecture that seminal virtues exuding with the water in the membranes of the neck were the cause of this strange generation.

[Thorndike, 8: 245]

John Dastin gives somewhat peculiar advice on what to do when a nursing infant whose mother has died is given to a wet nurse. This woman's hands are to be tied behind her back, and the child held in the appropriate nursing position—but watchfully, since "a great toad will spring from the milk and is to be slit through the middle and fed to a cock" [Thorndike, 3: 92]. For what purpose this is to be done is not made clear—it may be an alternate method of producing basilisks, or perhaps some now obscure allegorical meaning is intended.

Francis Bacon found that one could remove warts acquired by contact with toads by rubbing them with a bacon rind and then hanging the rind out of a window that faced south [Thorndike, 8: 196]. He also noted that the foulness of both air and soil around London during a plague outbreak was reflected by the toads, who were hopping about with tails two or three inches long [Thorndike, 7: 75–76]. The real barometric virtues of toads, however, were first recorded by Samuel Hartlib in the seventeenth century, when he wrote to Robert Boyle "concerning a weather prophet whose remarkably successful predictions were made by observing the changing colors of the skin of a toad which he kept in captivity" [Thorndike, 8: 197].

Toads occasionally made themselves useful in other ways, too. Albertus Magnus records how they were used to test the virtue of gems. The trick was to draw a circle around a toad using the gem in question, then to place the gem before the eyes of the now mesmerized toad. Within a matter of minutes either the gem, if flawed, would break apart, releasing the toad, or, if the gem were perfect, the toad would burst [Thorndike, 2: 546-47].

Perhaps the most positive and constructive act of the medieval toad, as widely denounced and vilified as it otherwise was during this period, was its internal production of an invaluable item known as the toadstone. Found in the heads of mature toads, this stone, perhaps by some mystical sympathy, would heat up or change color in the presence of poison. Set in a ring or worn about the neck, it could thus protect its wearer from foul play. Indeed, one author even recommends

AMERICAN
TOAD, BUFO AMERICANUS,
CLOSE-UP OF EYE
*Photo copyright 1983 by
Jeff Lepore
The National Audubon Society
Collection/Photo Researchers, Inc.
New York*

swallowing the toadstone if a person has already been poisoned, so that the stone "being down rolls about the bowels, and drives out every poisonous quality that is lodged in the intestines, then passes through the fundament, and is preserved," presumably for reuse [cited in Halliwell-Phillips, 6: 133]. Topsell confirms that "there be many that wear these stones in Rings, being verily persuaded that they keep them from all manner of gripings and pains of the belly and the smal guts" [Topsell: 727]. And Lloyd's *Treasure of Helth* extends the medical benefits to the treatment of kidney and bladder stones, the toadstone "being stampt and geven to the pacyent to drink in warme wine, maketh him to pise the stone out incontinent" [Cited in Halliwell-Phillips: 131].

"Sweet are the uses of adversity," says the old duke in *As You Like It*, "Which, like the toad, ugly and venomous,/Wears yet a precious jewel in his head." But just what this jewel was would be difficult to determine. Some literary scholars have suggested that Shakespeare must have been referring to the toad's beautiful eye—an interpretation that only reveals their ignorance of medieval toad lore. There does seem to have been some early confusion about whether the toadstone was actually a bone or a stone. Pliny had not mentioned a stone in writing of the virtues of certain toad bones, and Gesner records, in the sixteenth century, that the common people of England were partial to the toad's forehead bone [Halliwell-Phillips: 131]. Brasavolus, who went so far as to look inside a toad's head, claimed to have found no stone, only bone. This led someone else to suggest that perhaps the stone was contained inside a hollow toad bone. Topsell, in 1658, ends up recommending that curious persons settle the matter for themselves by doing a little dissection on their own.

Meanwhile, the mainstream of toadstone theory debated not the existence but only the nature and appearance of the stone,

> which is sometimes white, sometimes brown, or blackish, having a citrine or blew spot in the middle, sometimes all green, whereupon is naturally engraven the figure of a Toad, and this stone is sometimes called *Borax*, sometimes *Crapodinae*, and sometimes *Nisae*, or *Nusae*, and *Chelonites*. Others do make two kindes of these two stones, one resembling a great deal of milk mixed with a little bloud, so that the white exceedeth the red, and yet both are apparent and visible: the other all black, wherein they say is the picture of a Toad, with her legs spread before and behinde.   [Topsell: 721]

There was also some disagreement about the proper technique for procuring the stone. Lupton recommends bruising a large toad in various places, then placing it in an earthen pot and burying it in an anthill—the ants to eat everything but the bones and the precious stone [Halliwell-Phillips: 132]. But more sophisticated experts believed that when the toad died the virtue went out of the gem, which had to be procured from a living toad. Massarius outlines a surefire method for doing this: toads must be placed on a scarlet cloth,

> wherewithal they are much delighted, so that while they stretch out themselves as it were in sport upon that cloth, they cast out the stone of their head, but instantly they sup it up again, unlesse it be taken from them through some secret hole in the said cloth, whereby it falleth into a cistern or vessel of water, into which the Toad dareth not enter, by reason of the coldnesse of the water.   [Cited in Topsell: 727]

Porta refines the process slightly by stipulating that one must strike the toad so as to make it angry before it will give up its gem [Thorndike, 6: 283], and Lupton explains that one may be certain that the gem is the real thing if the toad leaps toward it and tries to snatch it back, since, "he envieth so much that man should have that stone" [Cited in Halliwell-Phillips: 132].

Nashe, in his *Anatomy of Absurdity,* refers to "the pearle which is affirmed to be in the head of the Toade" [cited in Robin, 1970], for which there is an intriguing parallel in the folklore of the Chinese: "the toad of Liu Hai produces during the night a pearl which, when eaten, changes a man into a saint or restores persons to life" [Eberhard: 205]. The *Kou Lou Shen Shu* contains the following prescription:

> One takes a big toad and fixes the four legs down with four iron nails over a foot long. The animal is then heated over a charcoal fire from dawn till noon. Then if one puts a cup of water in front of it, it will vomit a thing like a big soap-bean seed with a metallic lustre. Swallowed by people this magic seed will enable them to walk over rivers and lakes.
>
> [Read: 151]

Back on the European scene, the toadstone seems to have been most highly valued because of the popular practice of poisoning. By the principle of mystic sympathy or, put another way, fighting fire with fire, presumably the toadstone would register the presence even of toad poison. Thus the curious built-in antipathy recorded by Lyly, "the fayrer the stone is in the Toades head, the more pestilent the poyson is in hir bowelles" [cited in Robin: 136]. The fifteenth-century writer George Ripley describes the following believe-it-or-not experience with an ambivalently poisonous toad:

> *When busie at my booke I was upon a certeine night,*
> *The Vision here exprest appear'd unto my dimmed sight,*
> *A Toade full rudde I saw did drinke the juce of grapes so fast,*
> *Till over charged with the broth, his bowells all to brast;*
> *Thus drowned in his proper veynes of poysoned flood,*
> *For tearme of eightie dayes and fowre he rotting stood:*
> *By tryall then this venome to expell I did desire,*
> *For which I did committ his carkase to a gentle fire:*

Which done, a wonder to the sight, but more to be rehear'st,
The Toade with Colours rare through every side was pear'st,
And White appeared when all the sundry hewes were past,
Which after being tincted Rudde, for evermore did last.
Then of the venome handled thus a medicine I did make;
Which venome kills and saveth such as venome chance to take.
Glory be to him the graunter of such secret wayes,
Dominion, and Honour, both with Worship, and with Prayse.

[quoted in Thorndike, 4: 353]

Several medieval toad motifs come together in the following modern poem, ambivalent in its own way, by Conrad Hilberry. At first the toad seems sinister, associated with darkness, an object of fear. But its power is also seminal and organic: in the end, the darkness gives way to the rich colors of dawn, and the sun itself becomes the ultimate toadstone.

Toads

Dusk comes suddenly on the narrow road
that follows the hill eastward and down. The woman's
fears are the live pieces of dark that appear
where there was nothing.

In a tree that had been bare, she sees a dozen
great-tailed grackles slanting like eyebrows.
From a deserted hut comes a black feather of smoke
and a low voice.

Between the rocks, the dark is filling with toads:
their breath is the slow rising of the sky
behind her. She fears rain and she fears the toad-dust
thirsty for rain.

But then the evening sidles up to her,
holding out precious stones in a handkerchief.
She draws away from the opals and tigers' eyes,
sure that she will pay

ILLUSTRATION BY SEBASTIAN
FLEURET
from The Rhymes and Runes
of the Toad
by Susan Fromberg Schaeffer
Used by permission of Macmillan
Publishing Company
Illustration copyright 1975 by
Sebastian Fleuret
Photo by Judith DeGraaff

too much, but he touches her sleeve and she turns.
Below her in the rich light she sees a row
of trees like bubbles of blood welling up
from a cut

and beyond them the sky hunched like a toad
over the town, its skin mottled purple,
black, and vermillion. If this is the dark,
there is no escaping it.

She asks the name of the sky-toad, huge
and lovely. A tongue flickers from his mouth
and now the sun itself is a stone, burning
in his forehead.

                                    Conrad Hilberry

TOADS & WITCHCRAFT

A Visit to the Gingerbread House

"Why, sit down!" (So I let myself settle
In a fudge chair.) "I'll put on the kettle,"
Purred the witch. "Here, just try
Some delicious toad pie
And a cup of hot Hansel and Gretel!"

X. J. KENNEDY

Had George Ripley been an old woman, his intimacy with a toad, whatever his pious sentiments, might well have led to an accusation of witchcraft. During the Middle Ages and the Renaissance, and in folklore persisting into our own day, witches and toads have been closely connected. For one thing, as Topsell points out, "the women-witches of ancient time which killed by poysoning, did much use Toads in their confections" [Topsell: 730].

So did some of the men-witches, and they occasionally came to a bad end. Hugues Geraud, bishop of Cahors, admitted in 1317 to having made several attempts on the life of Pope John XXII "by poison and by sorcery with wax images, ashes of spiders and toads, the gall of a pig, and the like substances." Eventually he was "tortured and scourged with rods, burned at the stake, and his ashes were thrown into the Rhone" [Thorndike, 3: 18].

Social outcasts such as Jews, lepers, or witches were sometimes accused of attempting homicide on a much larger scale. In 1390, for example, under the reign of the French king Charles VI, "certain persons confessed under torture that they had poisoned the wells with the nails and flesh of corpses from the gibbet, the blood of a toad, and other impurities." The stated aim was "so that anyone drinking the water would gradually waste away and that in the course of time his hair would fall out and his skin come off at the touch of a hand" [Thorndike, 3: 926].

Considering that witches were supposed to be receiving direct assistance from the Devil himself, it is remarkable how often their worst intentions were thwarted. In Scotland in 1590, for example, Agnes Sampson and her company of nine other experienced witches seem to have followed their satanic master's instructions to the letter, but still James VI managed to escape scot-free. Melting a waxen image failed to harm him. Hanging a black toad up for nine days, roasting him, and catching his droppings turned out to be a lot of trouble for nothing when they were unable to obtain any of the king's underwear to dose with the poison [Wootton: 171, and Murray: 53].

Italian witchcraft was sometimes more romantically inclined. Cesalpino, in his *Peripatetic Questions*, records the tale of a young husband who was bewitched into leaving his wife and children. His affair was abruptly terminated, however, when his grieving spouse happened to look into the chamberpot, where she discovered a toad with its eyes sewn shut. When the toad had been duly cremated, her husband returned [cited in Thorndike, 6: 337]. Perhaps to destroy the toad was to destroy the witch; a more appealing symbolic interpretation, though, might be that it was only the husband's blind infatuation that was destroyed.

The activities of English witches were usually more mundane. They made their pact with the Devil in order to get the power to stop a neighbor's cows from giving milk, to procure a husband or render an enemy's husband impotent, to cause a variety of domestic accidents and bodily injuries, and generally to pester people they didn't like. They pledged a part of their bodies and/or souls, and were given in return one or more minor demons in the form of small animals, with which to work their wicked wills. These animals, called "imps" or "familiars," were kept in comfort and fed with bread, milk, and (on special occasions) drops of the witch's own blood. Thus damning evidence at

English witch trials was (1) any small animal kept as a pet, such as a mouse, cat, hare, dog, or toad (indeed, for the infamous witch-hunter Matthew Hopkins, a fly or spider anywhere in the room was sufficient) and (2) any special mark, sore, wen, or special extra teat on the witch's body from which milk or blood could be obtained to feed these familiars.

The first notable English trial for witchcraft occurred in 1566 at Chelmsford, Essex, and much of it concerned the antics of Elizabeth Francis's white spotted cat— Sathan by name— who occasionally took the form of a toad. Following the cat's directions, Elizabeth gave her body to a man she wanted as a husband, but later he refused to marry her. The cat then had rather more success in laying waste first the villain's goods, then his body, "whereof he died," and in giving Elizabeth an effective abortion recipe. The marriage strategy worked better on a second prospect, Francis, and this time the child was born. However, Elizabeth found she was not really cut out for motherhood, so she willed the cat to kill her baby, which it did. But things were still not quiet enough around the house, so she had the cat lame her husband in the following manner:

> It came in a morning to this Francis' shoe, lying in it like a toad; and when he perceived it, putting on his shoe, and had touched it with his foot, he being suddenly amazed asked of her what it was. And she bade him kill it, and he was forthwith taken with a lameness whereof he cannot be healed.
>
> [Robbins: 90]

Tiring of the cat some fifteen or sixteen years later, Elizabeth gave it to one Agnes Waterhouse, who changed it into a toad permanently because she needed the wool that lined its box [Robbins: 88–90].

In 1582, at the St. Osyth witch trials, Ursula Kempe's young son testified that one of her four familiars, a black toad named Pigin, had once caused a young child to become ill [Robbins: 191]. In 1599, Oliffe Barthram was executed for practicing devilish and wicked witchcraft upon one Joan Jordan, having sent three toads "to trouble her in her bed," and in 1574 Rachel Pindar claimed she was pestered by a familiar who appeared alternately as a dog and a toad [Kittredge: 182]. John Palmer confessed at St. Albans in 1649 that he had gone so far as to turn himself into a toad in order to torment one of his victims [Thomas, 1971: 517], and indeed, there often was an identification of witch and familiar, so that wounds inflicted upon the animal would later be found upon its owner.

Then there was a strange case, described by Joseph Glanvil in 1700, of the 1663 trial at Taunton of a seventy-year-old widow named Julian Cox. To establish that she was indeed a witch, one witness related a harrowing tale of a toad:

> That as he passed by Cox her Door, she was taking a Pipe of Tobacco upon the Threshold of her Door, and invited him to come in and take a Pipe, which he did, and as he was Smoking, *Julian* said to him, Neighbour, look what a pretty thing there is: He looked down and there was a monstrous great Toad betwixt his Legs, staring him in the Face: He endeavoured to kill it by spurning it, but could not hit it: Whereupon *Julian* bade him forebear, and it would do him no hurt; but he threw down his Pipe and went home (which was about two Miles off of *Julian Cox* her House) and told his Family what had happened, and that he believed it was one of *Julian Cox* her Devils.
>
> After, he was taking a Pipe of Tobacco at home, and the same Toad appeared betwixt his Legs: He took the Toad out to kill it, and to his thinking, cut it in several pieces, but returning to his Pipe, the Toad still appeared: He endeavoured to burn it, but could not: At length he took a Switch and beat it; the Toad ran several times about the Room to avoid him, he still pursuing it with Correction: At length the Toad cried, and vanished, and he was never after troubled with it.
>
> [Quoted in Kors and Peters: 306–307]

One's heart goes out to these old women, some of them probably senile, others deluded by their culture's superstitions into believing that they really were witches, most of them lonely and happy to share their dirt-floored huts with some local toad or mouse. At worst their crime may have been petty malice—yet for this they were accused, often tortured, sometimes hanged or burned to death. In legend and superstition, the witch with her toad friends remained the bugbear of the popular mind:

From a wild account of the murder of Fair Rosamond penned by an irresponsible chronicler of the fourteenth century . . . we learn that Queen Eleanor put Rosamond into a bath and hired a wicked old woman to lance her arms; and another old witch (sorceresse) brought two horrible toads, which seized the damsel's breasts and sucked her blood while two more hags held her arms. [Kittredge: 182–183]

These may be about the foulest of the toads and witches in English legend, but they can't hold a candle to their continental counterparts.

In Europe, from the early Middle Ages on, witches were identified with heretics; not only had they made a deal with the Devil, they had become his avowed worshipers, proponents of a religion counter to Christianity. Pope Gregory IX, in his bull of 1233, *Vox in Rama,* informs his bishops of the secret meetings of certain heretics:

> When a postulant wishes to become a member of their congregation, he is led into the midst of the meeting, whereupon the Devil appears in the form of a toad, goose, or duck, as a black cat with erect tail which descends a statue backwards to meet his worshipers, or as a thin, pale man with black, shining eyes. The postulant kisses the apparition either on the mouth or on the anus. When he has done, the master of the sect, and then the other initiates, also give the obscene kiss. After songs and a short liturgy, the lights are extinguished in order that a bisexual orgy may more comfortably occur.
> [Russell: 160–161]

With a few minor variations, the program for this meeting later became the typical agenda for a Sabbat, the midnight meeting of witches. At these midnight revels, the toad also figured prominently:

> Witches were especially fond of toads, pampering them as if they were children and dressing them in scarlet silk and green velvet capes for the celebration of the Sabbat. They wore bells around their necks and were baptized at the Sabbat.
> [Baskin: 320]

In 1329, a Carmelite monk, one Peter Recordi, was tried by the Inquisition at Carcassonne and condemned "for having made images of wax, toads' blood, and spittle, consecrating them to the Devil and then hiding them in the houses of women with whom he purposed sexual

THE MAGIC CIRCLE
John William Waterhouse
oil on canvas, 72" x 50", 1886
Tate Gallery (N1572), London
Art Resource, New York

In Waterhouse's painting, The Magic Circle, *a rather young and lovely witch, presiding over her bubbling cauldron, is about to complete a magic circle, whose purpose will be to summon the Devil. It is unclear whether the toad in the lower right will answer the summons as an embodiment of Satan, whether he is to be the next ingredient in the pot, or whether he is simply presiding over the ceremonies, along with the ravens, as an appropriately demonic animal.*

In Francken's The Witches' Kitchen *(late sixteenth century)*, *the nude woman on the far right is being rubbed with ointment, while other women begin to strip for the same treatment. On the far left a witch is already headed up the chimney on her broomstick. The toad seems to be trying to climb into the cauldron.*

▲ THE WITCHES' KITCHEN
H. Francken the Elder, 1540–1610
52 x 66 cm.
Gemäldegalerie,
KunsthistorischesMuseum, Vienna
SASKIA, Littleton, Colorado

Cornelius shows a number of witches approaching the Sabbat, some walking, others riding broomsticks or goats, guided by a radiant demon. They are properly attended by their familiars: rats, bats, owls, and demonic animal-composites. In the center foreground appears the inevitable toad, along with a lizard and some mushroom/toadstools. It looks like rather a long hop for a small toad.

THE WAY TO THE BROCKEN
illustration for Goethe's Faust
Peter Cornelius,
German, 1783–1867
Städelsches Kunstinstitut und
Städtische Galerie, Frankfort

intercourse" [Russell: 186]. But while there continued to be individual operators, European witchcraft seems generally to have been a group effort. A sect of Lyon, also indicted by the Inquisition, apparently held regular religious services to adore Satan, followed by feasts at which certain loathsome potions were drunk, the purpose being to keep everyone faithful:

> One of the accused, a woman named Bilia, admitted to having a familiar toad to which she fed meat, bread, and cheese and out of whose feces, together with human body hair, she made a powder from which she confected the potions drunk at the synagogues. [Russell: 223]

One had to be somewhat careful, since an overdose of this concoction could be fatal.

Ointments, salves, and various witchcraft potions throughout the Middle Ages, and after, might be taken by way of pledging the Devil or used to bring sickness or death to others. The ingredients, according to received opinion, make a rather grisly list. A recipe from Johannes Tinctoris (about 1460 A.D.) was

> to take toads to whom consecrated hosts have been fed, and kill them. Combine their flesh with the blood of murdered children, the bones of exhumed corpses, and menstrual blood, and mix well. [Russell: 240]

Of course witches thought nothing of murdering babies and small children, either to obtain ingredients for their potions, or merely to obtain a good meal.

Those herbs and "other things" are probably what put the kick into the witches' joy juice. To the toadskins were added botanical goodies from the world of solanaceous plants—henbane, mandrake, belladonna (deadly nightshade)—all powerfully hallucinogenic. Michael Harner

It would be hard to say whether or not Hieronymus Bosch ever hallucinated on witches' brew, but surely no painter has ever been more adept in picturing those inner demons of lust, guilt, revulsion, and fear embodied in witchlore. In the first of these two details from his large tryptich Last Judgment, *the king of Hell is framed in his doorway with a procession of toads.*

"KING OF HELL" DETAIL
FROM LAST JUDGMENT
*Hieronymus Bosch
Flemish, c. 1450–1515
Gemäldegalerie der Akademie der
bildenden Künste, Vienna*

In the second detail, depicting the punishment for gluttony, two reptilian-human figures seem to be cooking children. The hag, or witch, in the background is basting the head of a small child she is turning on a spit. Her squat figure, bulging belly, and skin covered with warts suggest a toad.

has accumulated a good deal of evidence from medieval records and earlier historians that salves of this sort were actually in use from the fourteenth century on. There was the case of Lady Alice Kyteler, for example, who was investigated by the authorities in 1324:

in rifleing the closet of the ladie, they found a Pipe of

"Gluttony"
detail from Last Judgment
Hieronymus Bosch
Flemish, c. 1450-1515
Gemäldegalerie der Akademie der
bildenden Künste, Vienna

The Devil himself once appeared to St. Anthony, according to the Vaderboek, *in the form of a toad with a human head [Bax: 40], and in this detail from Bosch's* Temptation of St. Anthony *three devils in the shapes of an ape, a dog, and a winged toad bear the long-suffering saint through the air in a horizontal position, the better to torment him. The toad seems to be sexually assaulting him from below, while nearby a young man exposes his rump and a second toadlike figure stands on its hands in demonic glee.*

oyntment, wherewith she greased a staffe, upon the which she ambled and galloped through thick and thin, when and in what manner she listed.   [Cited in Harner: 130]

Or as Bergamo notes in the fifteenth century:

the vulgar believe, and the witches confess, that on certain days or nights they anoint a staff and ride on it to the appointed place or anoint themselves under the arms and in other hairy places.   [Cited in Harner: 131]

A second detail, from the middle panel of the triptych, shows another toadlike figure, happily riding a winged coin—perhaps to Hell, perhaps to a Sabbat. Evidently the toad was a many-sided demon and could symbolize greed as well as lust or gluttony.

As Harner points out,

> the use of a staff or broom was undoubtedly more than a symbolic Freudian act, serving as an applicator for the atropine-containing plant to the sensitive vaginal membranes as well as providing the suggestion of riding on a steed, a typical illusion of the witches' ride to the Sabbat.   [131]

In addition to the auto-eroticism and the illusion of flight, the typical feature of broomride hallucinations was the sensation of being transformed into a bird or beast, the feeling that one's skin was being converted to fur, feathers, or a toad's warty hide. Thus it seems that many of the popular notions about witches—their animal transformations, broomstick flights, and orgiastic rituals—may have a biochemical explanation [Allen: 265–268].

DETAIL FROM THE
TEMPTATION OF ST.
ANTHONY
*Hieronymus Bosch
Flemish c. 1450-1515
Museu Nacional de Arte Antiga,
Lisbon
Photo by Mario Soares*

In the circle at the lower left in The Seven Deadly Sins and the Four Last Things, *Bosch associates the toad more particularly with female concupiscence (as did other painters of the period) by showing him perched upon a woman's pudenda.*

DETAIL FROM THE SEVEN
DEADLY SINS AND THE FOUR
LAST THINGS
*Hieronymus Bosch
Flemish, c. 1450–1515
Copyright Museo del Prado,
Madrid*

Harner suggests that an important difference between European witchcraft and Asian and New World shamanism, which obviously have much in common, is based on the difference in potency of the hallucinogenic drugs. The shaman was transported to the spirit world, but had to remain functional in the real world at the same time. But the massive assault on the central nervous system made by the solanaceous plants put witches into a comatose state, not only for the period of the trip, but for several days afterward. If witches wished to perform rites, combine their powers, or simply socialize, they did it at an Esbat, a sort of business meeting. The Sabbat, despite its congregational flavor, turns out to have been a purely individual experience [Harner: 146].

DETAIL "THE DAMNED" FROM
LAST JUDGMENT
Colijn de Coter
Dutch, 16th century
*collection of Wallraf-Richartz-
Museum, Cologne*
*Courtesy of Rheinisches Bildarchiv,
Cologne*

Colijn de Coter alters the position somewhat, placing the toad on the woman's breast.

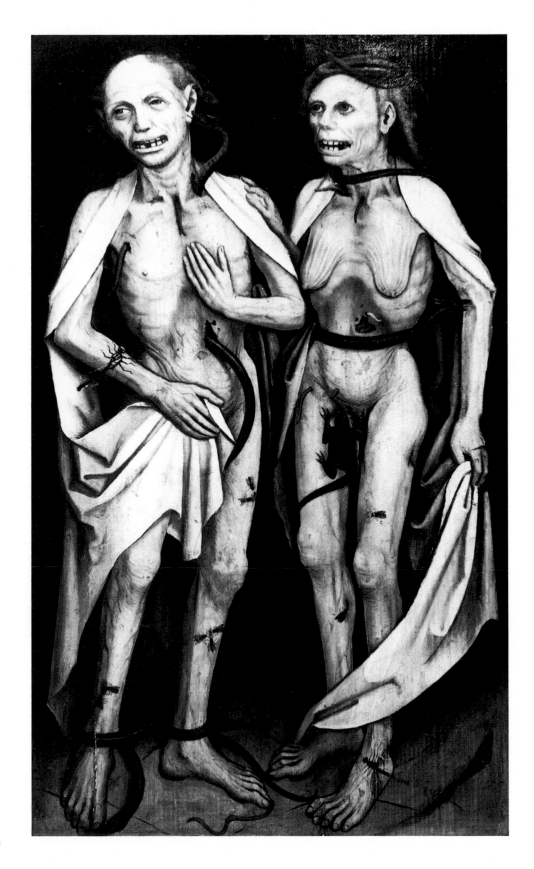

LES AMANTS TRÉPASSÉS
Maître des panneaux de Sterzing
Musée des Beaux-Arts Strasbourg, France.

The painter of Les Amants Trépassés *awards the toad a similar favored position, though here very much deromanticized.*

If any painter's imagination rivaled that of Bosch, it would have been that of Peter Brueghel the Elder. In his Dulle Griet, another world is falling apart, with the witchlike figure of "Mad Meg" headed for the Devil's gaping jaws, while toads emerge from the canal underworld.

DETAIL FROM **DE DULLE GRIET**
Peter Brueghel
Flemish, 16th century
Institut Royal du Patrimoine Artistique
Copyright A.C.L.-Brussels

Queen Elizabeth & the Frog/Toad Duke

This Frog he wou'd a Wooing ride . . .
With a Sword and Buckler by his side . . .
Traditional ballad

In a brilliant bit of historical detective work, Doris Adler has discovered how, back in Renaissance England during the reign of Good Queen Elizabeth, the frog and toad came to stand for sexual jealousy and has thereby explained the continued and intensified English animosity toward these hapless hoppers. For a number of years in the late sixteenth century, most seriously in the years 1579 through 1581, Elizabeth was being courted by the duke of Alençon. The queen may have seen an advantage in a French alliance, particularly for its potential assistance in combatting Spain and relieving the expense of her alliance with Holland; at any rate, she received the duke at her court, affectionately calling him her "frog." (The English did not begin referring to the French generally as "frogs" until the nineteenth century [Adler: 241].) Her many loyal Protestant subjects, however, despised this frog who came courting, both as a Frenchman—their bitterest traditional enemy—and as a Papist who was likely to plunge all England into subservience to that great whore of Babylon.

Thus one John Stubbs, in *The Discoverie of a Gaping Gulf*, 1579, "argued against the union with jealous fervor and referred to Elizabeth's frog as a 'venemous toad.' Stubbs had his right hand cut off, *The Gaping Gulf* was called in and destroyed, and any further expression of objections was forbidden" [Adler: 236–237]. Subsequently a myriad of references to frogs and toads, often with some direct or indirect reference to Catholicism or to France—but never with any open reference to the duke—began to appear in sundry writings of the anti-Alençon faction.

An early Greek mock heroic poem, *Batrachomyomachia* (Battle of the Frogs and Mice), saw its first English printing (as Latin verse) in early 1580. In it a frog, in trying to help a mouse across the water, actually drowns her; a war between the frogs and mice follows, which the mice are winning until Zeus sends the frogs some crab allies. The allegory of England's plight is obvious: "Elizabeth's frog may be trying to help, but that frog is a Catholic and the marriage could lead to civil war and powerful papal intervention" [Adler: 246].

In 1580 a traditional spinning song about a frog in a well and a mouse in a mill was licensed to Edward Hall under the title "A Moste Strange weddinge of the frogge and the mowse," and the same characters recur in Thomas D'Urfey's "A new Ditty on a high Amour at St. Jameses."

> *Great Lord Frog to Lady Mouse,*
> *Croakledom hee, Croakledom ho:*
> *Dwelling near St. Jameses House,*
> *Cocky mi Chari She;*
> *Rode to make his Court one day*
> *In the merry Month of May;*
> *When the Sun shon bright and gay.*
>
> *[reprinted in Shepard: 174]*

Other writers dropped the frog-mouse gambit and concentrated on the toad—perhaps as being more or less interchangeable in most people's minds, but having the more revolting appearance and foul reputation. Lupton begins his 1579 toad account "with Boccaccio's tale of the lovers who were killed by rubbing their teeth with sage that had been made poison at the root by the venomous breath of a great Toad" [cited in Adler: 250]. Bernard Garter, also in 1579, "warns all against

papists who like the 'venemous foule toade' cannot abide true doctrine."

Garter, however, goes further: not only are papists like toads, they used toads to poison English monarchs. Garter draws an analogy between the present threat to Queen and realm and the fate of King John, murdered with toad poisoning by a fanatic monk with the blessings and prior absolution of his abbott. [Adler: 248]

The great court stylist John Lyly had done nothing political with toads in *Euphues* (1578), but Adler finds covert satire in his sequel, *Euphues and His England* (1580), in which Lyly advises continental courtiers to steer clear of English ladies:

> I am of this mind with Homer, that as the snayle that crept out of hir shell was turned eftsoones into a Toad, and thereby was forced to make a stool to sit on, disdaining her own house; so the Travailer that stragleth from his own country, is in short tyme transformed into so monstrous a shape, that it is faine to alter his mansion, and to live where he canne, not where he would.   [Cited in Adler: 247]

John Stowe, in 1580, and Stephen Batman, in 1581, both

> repeat a story from Cambrensis of a young Welshman so persecuted by toads that his desperate friends were finally driven to place him in a coffin and hoist him to the top of a smooth and boughless tree, but to no avail; the toads pursued and ate him "to the bones that he dyed." Batman calls the young man "long legged Cecill" and describes him as having been "a great time visited with sicknesse," suggestions that bring to mind the Lord Treasurer, William Cecil, Lord Burghley, then an old man in poor health who supported the Elizabeth-Alençon alliance.   [Adler: 251]

Timothy Bright (1580) associates frog and toad poison with the French Pox [Adler: 252].

Overall, "of the miscellaneous secular texts and religious texts by laymen available for this three year period, 38 out of 70 include references to frogs and toads." However, the writings of state church-men, who had been warned off the subject, yield only one frog reference for the same period, and that one obscure [Adler: 249]. Obviously the anurans, after John Stubbs lost his hand, had become a hot political item.

In poetry, the toad load was carried by none other than Edmund Spenser. In the bleak December of *The Shepheardes Calender* (1579), Colin laments:

> *Wher I was wont to seeke the honey Bee,*

Working her formall rowmes in Wexen frame:
The grieslie Todestool growne there mought I see
And loathed Paddocks [toads or frogs] lording on the same.

[Cited in Adler: 257]

Negative toad imagery persists in *The Faerie Queen* (1590):

And next to him malicious Envie rode,
Upon a ravenous wolfe, and still did chaw
Betweene his cankred teeth a venemous tode,
That all the poison ran about his chaw . . .

Edmund Spenser, The Faerie Queene, *1.4.30*

The toad's new role as a symbol of sexual jealousy is made more clear in book 3, cantos 9 and 10. Here old Malbecco, jealous of his gold and of his wife's favors, ends up being robbed of both. In the climactic scene, he hides in the bushes fearing for his life, while one of the many satyrs his former bride now serves romps with her no fewer than nine times in a single night. When he at last slips in a word, she rejects him in favor of her new lovers. Nothing remains except to throw himself off a cliff, but he is so wasted away by jealousy that he merely floats to a safe landing below. Here he lives in a cave at the water's edge, the very embodiment of jealousy, and devoured by his inner demon:

Ne euer is he wont on ought to feed,
   But toades and frogs, his pasture poysonous,
   Which in his cold complexion do breed
   A filthy bloud, or humour rancorous,
   Matter of doubt and dread suspitious,
   That doth with curelesse care consume the hart,
   Corrupts the stomacke with gall vitious,
   Croscuts the liuer with internall smart,
And doth transfixe the soule with deathes eternall dart.

Edmund Spenser, The Faerie Queene, *3.10.59*

Shakespeare, born in 1564, was still a teenager during the Alençon affair, but when he began to write plays he also made ample use of negative toad imagery. His jealousy-toad haunts Othello (1604), who, convinced of Desdemona's infidelity, rants:

> *O curse of marriage,*
> *That we can call these delicate creatures ours,*
> *And not their appetites! I had rather be a toad*
> *And live upon the vapor of a dungeon*
> *Than keep a corner in the thing I love*
> *For others' uses.*

Othello, *3. 3. 268–273*

Later he feels the finger of infamy pointing him out for future generations, jeering at his most intimate conjugal feelings:

> *The fountain from the which my current runs*
> *Or else dries up—to be discarded thence,*
> *Or keep it as a cistern for foul toads*
> *To knot and gender in!*

Othello, *4. 2. 60–63*

But from his earliest plays, the Bard had been blackballing the toad in more traditional ways. In *Titus Andronicus* (c. 1590), a "blackamoor child" is described as "A joyless, dismal, black, and sorrowful issue!/... as loathsome as a toad" [4. 2. 66–67]. In *3 Henry VI* (c. 1591), Queen Margaret calls Richard "a foul mis-shapen stigmatic, / Mark'd by the destinies to be avoided / As venom toads, or lizards' dreadful stings" [2. 2. 136–138]. And in *Richard III* (c. 1591) we find the following rude exchange:

GLOUCESTER: Here. (She spits at him.) Why dost thou
> spit at me?
ANNE: Would it were mortal poison for thy sake!
GLOUCESTER: Never came poison from so sweet a place.
ANNE: Never hung poison on a fouler toad.
> Out of my sight! Thou dost infect mine
> eyes.

Richard III, *1. 2. 145–149*

The fairy queen herself, Elizabeth I, died in 1603, by which time the toad's reputation was at a very low ebb. Edward Topsell in his *History of Serpents* (1607), in summarizing the worst that had been thought and said of toads, found occasion both to rant against Catholi-

cism and, twice in two pages, to associate the toad with France: "I do marvel why in ancient time the *Kings* of France *gave in their Arms the three Toads in a yellow field*" [Topsell: 729].

Doris Adler, driven by Malbecco and Othello to go on this great Elizabethan toadhunt in the first place, suggests at the end of her essay that the jealousy-toad's apotheosis is not reached until *Paradise Lost*, in 1667, when "Milton chose as the very form of Satan's cosmic jealousy a toad crouching at the ear of Eve" [Adler: 260]:

> . . . *Him there they found*
> *Squat like a toad, close at the ear of Eve,*
> *Assaying by his devilish art to reach*
> *The organs of her fancy, and with them forge*
> *Illusions, as he list, phantasms and dreams.*
> *Or if, inspiring venom, he might taint*
> *The animal spirits, that from pure blood arise*
> *Like gentle breaths from rivers pure, thence raise,*
> *At least, distempered, discontented thoughts,*
> *Vain hopes, vain aims, inordinate desires,*
> *Blown up with high conceits engendering pride.*
>
> Paradise Lost, *Book 4, 799–809*

For more than forty years Milton scholars have debated whether Satan actually took a toad's shape himself, took temporary possession of an actual toad's body, or simply miniaturized his own angelic form and squatted to get better access to Eve's unconscious mind via her ear canal. Whatever Milton had in mind, the negative connotations of toadness would all work well here. For one thing, there was the traditional witchcraft connection between toad and Devil, both in Satan's appearance as a great toad to be kissed by initiates and in the toad-familiar minor demons. For another, the toad's supposed power to poison with its breath appears in the phrase "inspiring venom," for Milton no doubt intends "inspiring" in its literal Latin sense of "breathing into." So, as God had originally breathed into man the breath of life, Satan now tries to breathe into woman the breath of death. Though Toad-Satan's motivation may include jealousy, the squatting toad also suggests earlier toad emblems of anger and revenge, of squalid lust ("inordinate desires") and swelling pride.

Toad Folk & Fairy Tales

Speculating on what it feels like to be a prince,
Prince Dmitri of Yugoslavia confessed, "I can't
really say—I've never been a toad."

San Francisco Examiner, *7 March 1984*

The toad-duke of Alençon was already a duke when he came a-courting Queen Elizabeth, but the transformation of a toad or frog to a prince becomes important in children's fairy tales of succeeding centuries. The ugly hag, in these stories, may be revealed as a lovely maiden when the witch's spell is broken, or she may assume her true beauty only when treated with kindness. Similarly, the loathsome toad, marvelously metamorphic, needs only to be kissed to turn into a charming, amiable, and in-every-way-desirable prince. In confronting the arbitrary and inscrutable world, a child learns that all things bright and beautiful are not always good things; and ugliness is no longer automatically evil, but may be good in disguise. Nor, if the right magic can be found—the right word spoken, or the right deed enacted—is one doomed to remain in poverty, powerlessness, and squalor.

The toad in "The Three Feathers," a Grimm tale, plays a key role in engineering transformations. She is large, fat, and female, with her subterranean headquarters practically beneath the king's castle. With her myriad offspring, she may suggest an Ur-toad earthmother figure—*yin* driven underground—or at least some version of the house-toad of German tradition, who "lives in the cellar of the house and through its influence keeps the food stuffs that are stored there wholesome; through this, prosperity comes to the house, and the animal is called, therefore, treasure-toad" [cited in Gubernatis: 380, n.1; translation from the German by Nils Ekfelt].

The story begins when the king, grown old and weak, must decide which of his three sons should inherit the kingdom. The two oldest seem very clever and articulate, but the youngest doesn't say much and is generally regarded as a simpleton. What follows, of course, is the inevitable three-part test of worthiness. The king takes the boys outside and flips three feathers into the air to determine which directions his sons will take in seeking the most beautiful carpet. One feather flies east, and one flies west, but Simpleton's flies straight up and then flutters to the ground. The two older sons, in the arrogance of their worldly wisdom, think the coarse handkerchiefs they bring back will be more than enough to beat out Simpleton. But Simpleton, looking deeper into the nature of things, discovers a trapdoor at his feet, with stairs leading into the earth. These bring him into the presence of the Great Toad, with all her little ones, and a huge box containing every good and perfect gift, including a carpet so beautiful and fine that no one on earth could have woven it.

Having won the first contest, Simpleton goes on to triumph in the second test, for the procuration of a beautiful ring is no great challenge for the toad either. But the final test appears more difficult—to bring back the most beautiful woman. The older brothers bring back coarse peasant women, but Simpleton reenters the bowels of the earth to put his fortunes in the horny hands of his toad-mother mentor. When he follows her directions and places one of the little toads, selected at random, into a hollow turnip that is harnessed to six mice, the Cinderella transformation occurs and he finds himself sporting a coach and six, complete with beautiful maiden. He kisses her to seal the bargain and is subsequently pronounced the winner by the king.

Now the older brothers insist on testing the validity of the women by making them jump through a hoop. The peasant women are strong but clumsy, and end up breaking their legs, while the toad-maiden, no longer an ungainly hopper, springs nimbly through. Thus all opposition to Simpleton's reign is brought to an end [based on Stern: 319–322].

Bruno Bettelheim suggests that the seemingly inept Simpleton in tales like "The Three Feathers," invariably the youngest in the group, represents the self-concept of a child in a threatening grown-up world. The descent to the toad-underworld, in this particular tale, suggests a descent into the unconscious, resulting in a psychic wholeness never achieved by the older brothers:

> what enables Dummy to win out is his reliance on his animal nature, the simple and primitive forces within us. The toad is experienced as an uncouth animal, something from which we do not normally expect refined products. But this earthy nature, when well used for higher purposes, proves itself far superior to the superficial brightness of the brothers, who take the easy way by remaining on the surface of things.
>
> . . . .
>
> Becoming familiar with the unconscious . . . is necessary but not sufficient. Acting on these insights must be added; we must refine and sublimate the content of the unconscious. That is why, the third and last time, Dummy himself has to choose one of the little toads. Under his hands the turnip turns into a carriage, the mice into horses. And, as in many other fairy tales, when the hero embraces—that is, loves—the toad, it turns into a beautiful girl. It is, in the final analysis, love which transforms even ugly things into something beautiful.
> [Bettelheim: 107–108, 110]

The transformation, then, represents psychic wholeness: in Bettelheim's terms, it involves a sorting out of elements of the ego—a coming to terms with one's animal nature. This process also includes moral development:

> Man's relationship to the toad or, in an individual, the ego's relationship to the toad archetype, is of great importance because, since *Bufo* is potentially a midwife, it is, if understood, capable of bringing to birth a new consciousness. This is, however, only likely to happen if the ego's attitude is right, for, according to the fairy stories, it is through the voluntary sacrifice, by human beings, of disgust and contempt, that this

dark and ugly little creature may emerge from the depths and
be transformed into shining royalty.   [Dale-Green: 25]

But what is going on here may be even more complicated (or different)
than that. Since the toad-to-maiden or toad-to-prince transfiguration
results in the finding of a mate, it is hard to ignore its sexual implications.
Is "The Three Feathers" in reality a tale of female potency, couched in
sexual terms, invading and undermining the male-dominated castle?

Or does the beauty-beast dichotomy symbolize adolescent ambivalence toward puberty? In one sense, coming to terms with the toad-
id may be seen as accepting one's own sexuality. The frog/toad may
seem both foreign and slimy, but, accepted into the young girl's bed and
embraced, it becomes the delightful prince, her husband: "even an
animal so clammily disgusting turns into something very beautiful,
provided it all happens in the right way at the right time" [Bettelheim:
290].

Daughters With Toad

Unblinking thing, as absolute as clay.
Fumed from the dank by my mower's snarl, he muses.
My daughters find him, and their squeals propel,
bounce him from his mope, ringing him with glee.

With sly, leary touch they probe his apathy
unearthed—half-thrown, with lurching, bloated thump
he falls. They toy and stroke, forgive his piss,
his pebbled hide, coo to his bulbous stare.

Squat in their palms, he thrills them with his pulse.
They lean near, enraptured by his ugliness,
wild hair burnished down round him in bright waves.
And they whisper, foreheads almost touching.

Then each brings her lips to meet that grim crack
of torpid mouth. They return him to grass
to wait the kisses' transformation.
Nothing. The pale throat only swells the air

and flutters, emits one pathetic croak.
They laugh, and to the toad, their teeth so fine

must gleam like the teeth of little foxes.
Uneaten, he ponders on, abandoned.

My daughters are not sad. The day will be
husband enough, obedient to whim—
a royal ball. They waltz toward lunchtime,
assuring me he spoke to them in prince.

Mark Defoe

The true nature of toad-prince communication may be revealed in a variant of the familiar "Beauty and the Beast" tale from the Schoharie Hills of New York State, "The Rose Story." A rich farmer, forced to travel to look after his investments, asks each of his three daughters what sort of gift she would like him to bring back. The older girls request a silk dress and a fancy fan, but the youngest wants nothing but her father's safe return; when pressed, she asks only for a rose.

Some months later, his fortune preserved, the farmer returns, dress and fan in hand but waiting to pick the rose until he is near home so that it will be fresh. Ironically, this simplest request proves the most fateful for no roses are to be had; and when he finally finds one and picks it, a headless man rises out of the ground and demands a penalty—either the farmer must give his life, or his youngest daughter must live forever in the house of the headless man. The unfortunate father decides that he must pay the piper, but obtains permission to go home to drop off his gifts and say good-bye. But the young girl, now grown into a lovely maiden, manages to uncover her father's secret and, out of love for him, determines to pay the price herself. Despite her fears, she rises early the next day, steals his horse, and rides to meet her ordeal.

Things begin quietly enough at the monster's house as she finds a bright fire burning on the hearth and a breakfast table laid for two. It turns out that breakfast is actually brought in not by the dreaded headless man but by a giant toad. The toad proves to be a domestic wizard, serving up three square meals a day, cleaning up the dishes, and keeping the fire blazing quite cheerily. Somewhat disquietingly, it shares her bed as well as her meals, but otherwise maintains its silent and harmless habits.

One day the young maiden, lonely and homesick, walks out to the garden and picks a rose, thus resurrecting the headless one. From him

she obtains permission for a quick visit home, but she must submit to the continued companionship of the huge toad, who now rides behind her in the saddle.

At last, however, her instincts lead her to a solution to the problem. For the first time she keeps her eyes open when the toad invades her bedroom, and when she sees him slip out of his thick, warty skin, revealing a handsome, well-dressed young man, she seizes the skin and destroys it in a kettle of boiling water. The spell of the witch, his jealous would-be lover, is destroyed along with the headless monster, and

THE PRINCESS AND THE
FROG
Mary Shepard Greene
Blumenschein (1869–1958)
oil on panel, 64.3 x 81 cm.
1909
The Brooklyn Museum, 18.44
Gift of the Brooklyn Woman's
Club in memory of
Mrs. Mary I. Greene

wedding bells complete the breaking up of the old gang [based on Gardner: 118–123].

If "The Rose Story" is sexually symbolic, its implications are a little hard to sort out. It might seem that sexuality is being forced upon the young maiden by a male-dominated world (the farmer, the headless creature, and the giant toad). But behind it all lies the power of the young witch whose desire for the handsome young man had been thwarted. It might be posited, in Bettelheim's terms, that the pubescent girl is learning to accept her own sexuality; or is it sexual otherness that she accepts? It might even be argued that the story implies a rejection of sexuality: a monster presides over the house of initiation, and the male is hideous until his toad skin is actually destroyed, when he emerges well and fully dressed. Nor does any embrace occur in the rose house—wedding bells are to ring later, back in a more domestic setting.

In the following modern poem, by contrast, no bells ever do ring:

Toad

Seated on well-lip
toad and lady,
blotched skin, thin tongue
flicking at flies,
white skin, round flank,
eyes of compassion
and dry-mouthed hunger
thought to kiss.

Who, save in the
nightmare of country
wisdom, would earn
the wart on the lip
for hope of the jewel?
As she bent down
the moon was hidden,
the trees stood still.

Here was her fortune.
Her heart shook.
Her small breasts trembled
within her gown.

Her breath was musky.
She bit her lip.
Unblinking, the toad
watched her stoop down

then leapt into darkness.
He was darkness.
Lover, she cried, Ah Lover
as she fell,
the moonlit well-head above her
bright as a jewel,
the leap of her tongue
an echo down the well

of every darkness
gathered in every need.
They found her at morning,
head split by a stone.
There is no prince in this country,
only mirrors
kissing within the darkness
where we drown.

Robin Skelton

In this twentieth-century poem the magic has departed; no transformations are possible. We are trapped within ourselves, without insight or communication: no human voices wake us, and we drown in the toad-darkness. To make its nihilistic point, Skelton's "Toad" reverses the implications of a fairy tale like "Toads and Diamonds," where the young, beautiful sister's kindness to the hag is rewarded when her very words are turned to flowers and jewels (which attract her prince), while the ugly and cranky older sister is made to speak literal toads and snakes; she dies alone in a corner of the woods [see Opie and Opie: 100–102].

The toad's role in fairy tales, then, seems important but mixed: in some tales, the medieval and Renaissance connection with ugliness and evil is continued, while in others the toad seems to enter a new alliance with positive psychic forces. In many *folk* tales, however, where the symbolic load is generally less burdensome, the toad is often perceived as an amiable, even appealing, character.

This is certainly the case in a lighthearted Jamaican variation of the old tortoise-and-hare story, recorded in dialect by W. Jekyll in 1966. Here the king sets up a twenty-mile race between a toad and a donkey. The "trickified" toad gets a twenty-four-hour delay before the start of the race, during which time he plants one of his children at each of the twenty mile posts. The confident donkey begins the race slowly, munching grass and peas for at least an hour on his way to the first milepost; but here, when he bawls out "Ha! Ha! Ha! me more than Toad," he is answered by an invisible toad child, "Jin-ko-ro-ro, Jin-kok-kok-kok." Not too concerned at first, the donkey begins increasing his speed, but as his boast is thrown back at him at each succeeding milepost, he becomes desperate and soon gallops himself out. When he concludes that he has lost the race, we get the moral of the story: "through Toad smartness Donkey can never be racer again" [Jekyll: 39–42].

The lowly toad also triumphs in an African toad tale told by Kombo Banda of the Gbaya and recorded in 1967 in Bouli (Cameroun). Here there are no magical transformations for the toad-suitor. The lovely maiden and her family prefer the slick-skinned frog (Fulani man) to the ugly warty toad (black Gbaya man), but the toad-man proves to be the only successful hunter. The girl ends up eating spinach prepared by her mother, when she might have had elephant steak. In Africa, as elsewhere, beauty is only skin-deep [Dorson: 492-498].

Note: For a modern Fairy tale in which the toad-prince or prince toad at last attains triumphant fairy-tale apotheosis, without benefit of metamorphosis, see Howard McCord's "The Great Toad Hunt" reprinted in Appendix A.

THE ENDURING TOAD

*Toads are tamping down cakes of moss
where Potter's Lake pocks the yellow grass.*

DAVE ETTER, "FIREWOOD HILL"

Bufophiles may rejoice: not only have centuries of abuse failed to wipe out the toad, but there are even signs in modern times of a trend to clear his good name. Meanwhile, it is surprising to see how long it has taken science to supplant superstition, particularly among the folk. In 1850 the literary periodical *Notes and Queries* reported that "an English spell for black magic . . . was to hang up nine living toads on a string and then bury them: as they pine away, your enemy will languish until death comes" [cited in Kittredge: 95]. A Shropshire woman who kept a box of live toads in her cottage was murdered in 1857 [Kittredge: 182]. "In 1879 in Norfolk a man accused of assaulting a girl defended his action on the ground that her mother had bewitched him by means of 'a walking toad'" [Kittredge: 47; the toad must have been a natterjack]. In 1900, *Folk-lore* recorded the case of an old woman in Devonshire who "kept toads in her back kitchen for the purpose of injuring persons against whom she had a grudge; another, who was bedridden, kept toads in her bed, and people used to come to have their fortunes told by them" [cited in Kittredge: 182]. *The Antiquarian* for 1905 stated that "there were witches in Devon who professed to be able and willing to torture anybody by means of a sheep's heart or a toad full of pins hung up in the chimney" [cited in Kittredge: 99].

Some poets and writers of the nineteenth and early twentieth centuries have scarcely been any kinder to *Bufo*. In *Pierre* (1852), Herman Melville seems to argue that man's sexual nature is his doom, shaking down all his higher aspirations; ideal love is haunted by the foul "toads and scorpions" of lust [Kellner: 19–20]. In one of George Eliot's first stories, *Janet's Repentance* (1857), the brutal alcoholic Robert Dempster falls out of his gig and is carried home. As his long-suffering wife, Janet, attends his bedside, Robert raves in delirium:

> Your blood is yellow . . . in your purse . . . running out of your purse . . . What! you're changing it into toads are you? They're crawling . . . they're flying . . . they're flying about my head . . . the toads are flying about. Ostler! ostler! bring out my gig . . . bring it out, you lazy beast . . . ha! you'll follow me, will you? . . .you'll fly about my head . . . you've got fiery tongues . . . Ostler! curse you! why don't you come? Janet! come and take the toads away . . . Janet!

It seems clear that the chief engineer of the *Patna*, in Joseph Conrad's *Lord Jim* (1900), is also tormented by toad-demons of guilt in his *delirium tremens* (chapter 5). His pink toads, Ian Watt suggests [274], represent the so-called "pilgrims" whom he and the *Patna* have deserted:

> Millions of pink toads. It's worse than seeing a ship sink . . . . The ship was full of them. They've got to be watched, you know . . . . All pink. All pink—as big as mastiffs, with an eye on the top of the head and claws all round their ugly mouths. Ough! Ough!

Perhaps Christopher Ricks is right in thinking that Conrad borrowed these toad-demons from George Eliot. Dempster was being tended by a Dr. Pilgrim, so the toad-guilt-pilgrim connection is there in both cases [Ricks: 143]. And earlier in Conrad's chapter the *Patna's* master had had a stormy interview with a Captain Elliot. (Is this the stuff that literary symbolism is made of?)

Freudian literary toad-critics may find their happiest hunting ground in the short story "Toad," probably written about 1910 by Geza Csath, a Yugoslavian neurologist, opium addict, litterateur, and early suicide. The narrator, who is reminiscent of some of Edgar Allen Poe's demented storytellers, is forced by his nightmares into a revolting and violent intimacy with a hairy toad the size of a cat, which invades his kitchen. Seeking to protect his wife from this creature of ill omen, he withstands its ghastly sounds, its miasmic stench, and even its biting attack on his neck, finally chopping it up with a hatchet until only a "slimy and foul green mass" remains. Next morning no traces of the loathsome battle adorn the kitchen floor, but within two weeks the narrator's beloved wife is dead.

Psychologically, the displacement of feelings of revulsion and violence from wife to toad seems pretty obvious here. But what is most striking about the story is the intensity of loathing with which the toad is described: seldom has so vile a creature haunted the human imagination.

Another short-lived and toad-tormented spirit was the French proto-surrealist Isidore-Lucien Ducasse (1846-1870), who penned, under the pseudonym Comte de Lautréamont, the anguished prose-poem *Les Chants de Maldoror* (1868). In the canto beginning "The brother to the leech paced slowly through the forest," Maldoror addresses *frère crapaud* (brother toad) in the following demented fashion:

> "Who is that being, there on the horizon, who dares approach me fearlessly with tormented, oblique leaps? And what majesty, mingled with serene mildness! His look, though soft, is profound. His enormous eyelids frolic in the breeze, and seem alive. He is beyond my ken.
>
> "Meeting his monstrous eyes, my body quakes—for the first time since I sucked the dry dugs of what one calls a mother. There is a sort of halo of dazzling light about this being. When he spoke, all nature was stilled, and shared in a huge shudder. Since it pleases you to come to me, as if drawn by a magnet, I've no objection to that. How handsome he is! It pains me to say so. You must be strong, for you have a

superhuman countenance, sad as the universe, beautiful as suicide. I abhor you to the utmost, and would rather see a serpent coiled round my neck from time immemorial than miss your eyes. . . .

"What! . . . It's you, toad! . . . Fat toad! . . . Ill fated toad! . . . Forgive me! . . . Forgive me! . . . Why are you on this earth where the accursed are? But what have you done to your viscous, foetid pustules that you should have so sweet a look? When, by a higher command, you came down from above on a mission to comfort the various breeds of existing creatures, you swooped upon earth with the speed of a kite, wings unwearied by this long, splendid errand. I saw you! Poor toad! How I mused then on the infinite, as well as on my frailty. 'One more being,' I told myself, 'who is superior to those on earth; and that by divine will. Why not I too? What place has injustice in the supreme decrees? Is the Creator mad? He is, though, the strongest, and his wrath terrible!' Since you appeared to me, monarch of marshes and ponds, clad in a glory that belongs only to God, you have, in some measure, consoled me. But my wavering wits are engulfed by such majesty! Who are you? Stay . . . Oh! stay longer on this earth! Fold your white wings, and do not look upward with anxious eyes . . . If you leave, let us leave together!"

[trans. Lykiard: 31–32]

Clearly the poet-toad identification is not a happy one: Lautréamont seems to assume feelings of disgust and revulsion toward toads, which he uses for shock value in embracing the toad as alter ego.

The humanization of the French toad is less painful in J. J. Grandville's *Public and Private Life of Animals* (1842). Grandville (Jean Ignace Isidore Gérard) was an illustrator who specialized in insects, birds, and reptiles. The whimsical text of the work, contributed by various hands, seems to have been furnished mainly as a vehicle for the illustrations. One story entitled "The Sorrows of an Old Toad," offers the following autobiographical musings:

My father was already well up in years and corpulence, when the joys of paternity came upon him for the last time. Alas! his happiness was of short duration. My poor mother's strength was overtaxed with a dreadful laying of eggs, and, in spite of

the tenderest nursing, she at last succumbed to the effort of bringing me to the light. I was brought forth in sorrow, and to this fact I attribute the deep shade of melancholy which has clouded my existence. I was always of a dreamy, contemplative nature. This, indeed, formed the basis of my character. The early days of my Tadpole life are wrapped in gloom, so dense as to render them void of incident. I can just dimly recollect my father, squatted beneath a broad leaf on the bank of a stream, smiling benignly as he watched my progress. He

ILLUSTRATION FOR PUBLIC
AND PRIVATE LIFE OF
ANIMALS
J.J. Grandville
1877
Photo by Edward Pierce

had always a soft, liquid eye, in whose depths I could read the
love of his tender heart. His eyes were of a greenish hue, and
protruded. This, taken together with his noble proportions,

ILLUSTRATION FOR PUBLIC
AND PRIVATE LIFE OF
ANIMALS
J.J. Grandville
1877
Photo by Edward Pierce

his enemies attributed to high living. He was in reality a contemplative Toad, whose greatest success lay in the cultivation of philosophic leisure. He carefully avoided the water, and, little by little, withdrew himself from the scene of my exploits. I am ashamed to say that his absence never caused me to shed a tear.

The young tadpole pursues the pleasures of idyllic underwater life until his painful metamorphosis into a toad. Rude encounters with a goose and her goslings, a kingfisher, and a porcupine soon teach him to see himself as an ugly and revolting creature, which doesn't stop him from risking his life to save a grasshopper to whom he has lost his heart. But his only reward is mockery from the delicate grasshopper and her friends. The story ends:

> There would be no plain-looking or even ugly creatures to curse the day of their birth, were there no cruel, well-favoured observers to wound them with their looks and gestures. But I am forgetting the lesson which I myself learned late in life. I had put myself in the way of finding out by experience that a poor toad could never have wings, nor, though everything is fair in love and war, could he hope to win the heart of a grasshopper.
>
> I am now full of years and philosophy; my wife, like myself, is a contemplative full-bodied toad, in whose eyes I am perfectly beautiful. I must own my appearance has greatly improved. The like compliment cannot be honestly paid to my mother-in-law, who has caused me no small trouble. She increases in age and infirmities. The reader will pardon my repeating, that notwithstanding my rotundity, I am no longer ugly. Should he have any doubt on this point, let him ask my wife! [trans. Thompson, 1877: 63, 73]

The inimitable Henri de Toulouse-Lautrec, a few years later, imported a toad to serve as a model for the illustration "Le Crapaud" that he contributed to his friend Jules Renard's *Histoire Naturelles;* we know that he fed it and gave it free run of his Paris studio, and that he felt some regret when it disappeared.

Ungainly Things

A regular country toad—pebbly,
*   squat,*
*   shadow-green*

as the shade of the spruces
*   in the garden*
*   he came from—rode*

Le Crapaud
plate twelve from Jules Renard's
Histoires Naturelles
(H. Floury, Paris)
Henri de Toulouse-Lautrec
lithograph, printed in black comp:
31.6 x 22.5 cm. (irreg.)
1899
Collection, The Museum of Modern
Art, New York
The Louis E. Stern Collection

to Paris in a hatbox
to Lautrec's
studio (skylights

on the skies of Paris)
and stared
from searchlight eyes,

dim yellow; bow-armed
ate
cutworms from a box

hopped
occasionally
among the furniture and easels,

while the clumsy little painter
  studied
      him in charcoal

until he was beautiful.
  One day
      he found his way

down stairs toward the world
  again,
      into the streets of Montmartre,

and, missing him, the painter-dwarf
  followed,
      peering among cobbles,

laughed at, searching
  until long past dark
      the length of the Avenue Frochot,

over and over,
  for the fisted, marble-eyed
      fellow

no one would ever see again
  except
      in sketches that make
        ungainly things
          beautiful.

                          Robert Wallace

For Apollinaire, writing to Louise de Coligny from the front in the First World War, the toad seems to have lost all of its negative connotations:

> . . . at night there is a toad which rings out a note pure and clear, like the moonlight scattered over the battlefields . . .
> [letter of 2 May 1915]

. . . .

My little love, the toads and the baby toads sing a single note

which is like the burned topaz of your eyes and which says
"Lou, Lou, Lou . . . ." (letter of 4 June 1915);

[trans. Scott Bates]

Meanwhile, the British toad's reputation had steadily gained
ground throughout the nineteenth century, as if in reflection of
communal response to a popular metaphor, "the toad under the
harrow." Its initial reference was to farm laborers (who no doubt had
themselves unearthed many a toad with their cultivators), as a variant
on the too-many-chiefs-and-not-enough-Indians motif; thus the Scotch
proverb "the toad said to the harrow, 'Cursed be so many lords,' "
adapted by Thomas Fuller in his *Gnomologia* (1732) to "Too many
Masters, quoth the Toad to the Harrow, when every Tine turned her

over." Sir Walter Scott appropriately puts the line into the mouth of a cranky Scotch gardener in *Rob Roy* (1818):

> To the commands of Mr. Jarvie, therefore, Andrew was compelled to submit, only muttering between his teeth, "Ower mony maisters—ower mony maisters, as the paddock said to the harrow, when every tooth gae her a tig."
>
> [Scott: 253]

Later, in the writings of Jeremy Bentham, Samuel Smiles, and others, the metaphor was regularly and sympathetically applied to anyone living humbly and enduring hardships as the price of ultimate success. In *Departmental Ditties* (1886), Rudyard Kipling points the proverb poetically in "Pagett, M.P." The speaker in the poem is a veteran of the Indian service whom a smug Parliamentary visitor regards as underworked and overpaid. Pagett initially pooh-poohs the problems of life in India, but after being persuaded to stay on there through the summer, succumbs to the insects, the diseases, and the heat—and so the speaker is vindicated in the end. The poem's epigraph reads as follows:

> *The toad beneath the harrow knows*
> *Exactly where each tooth point goes.*
> *The butterfly upon the road*
> *Preaches contentment to that toad.*
>
> *Rudyard Kipling*

Robert Browning sometimes shows a decidedly Shakespearian hostility to toads, referring to "toads in a poisoned tank" in "Childe Roland to the Dark Tower Came," and numbering toads among the harmful creatures removable by the Pied Piper. But even he adopts the sympathetic toad metaphor in "Instans Tyrannus" (1845), where the poor wretch, a "toad or rat" to the cruel tyrant who oppresses him, finds God on his side at the last. It turns out that Browning had had a toad friend in his youth:

> He visited it daily where it burrowed under a white rosetree, announcing himself by a pinch of gravel dropped into its hole;

and the creature would crawl forth, allowing its head to be gently tickled, and reward the act with a loving glance of its soft full eyes.

[Mrs. Orr, cited in Scudder: 989, and Ortega: 79]

The toad returns as a sort of alterego for the poet in a whimsical poem called "White Witchcraft," published, by an odd coincidence, on the day of Browning's death in 1889:

> *If you and I could change to beasts, what beast should either be?*
> *Shall you and I play Jove for once? Turn fox then, I decree!*
> *Shy wild sweet stealer of the grapes! Now do your worst on me!*
>
> *And thus you think to spite your friend—turned loathsome? What, a*
>   *toad?*
> *So, all men shrink and shun me! Dear men, pursue your road!*
> *Leave but my crevice in the stone, a reptile's fit abode!*
>
> *Now say your worst, Canidia! "He's loathsome, I allow:*
> *There may or may not lurk a pearl beneath his puckered brow:*
> *But see his eyes that follow mine—love lasts there, anyhow."*
>
> *[ed. Scudder: 989]*

As Emily Dickinson, on the other side of the Atlantic, had already pointed out, "A Toad, can die of Light—/Death is the Common Right/of Toads and Men." The lesson here is humility: "Why swagger, then?/The Gnat's supremacy is large as Thine" [ed. Johnson: 285].

The same lesson is writ somewhat larger by Archy the cockroach in Don Marquis's *The Lives and Times of Archy and Mehitabel:*

warty bliggens, the toad

> *i met a toad*
> *the other day by the name*
> *of warty bliggens*
> *he was sitting under*
> *a toadstool*
> *feeling contented*
> *he explained that when the cosmos*
> *was created*

that toadstool was especially
planned for his personal
shelter from sun and rain
thought out and prepared
for him

do not tell me
said warty bliggens
that there is not a purpose
in the universe
the thought is blasphemy
a little more
conversation revealed
that warty bliggens
considers himself to be
the center of the said
universe
the earth exists
to grow toadstools for him
to sit under
the sun to give him light
by day and the moon
and wheeling constellations
to make beautiful
the night for the sake of
warty bliggens

to what act of yours
do you impute
this interest on the part
of the creator
of the universe
i asked him
why is it that you
are so greatly favored

ask rather
said warty bliggens
what the universe
has done to deserve me
if i were a
human being i would

not laugh
too complacently
at poor warty bliggens
for similar
absurdities
have only too often
lodged in the crinkles
of the human cerebrum

        archy

Perhaps the mixed literary legacy of *Bufo* in our time is best demonstrated by the late great British poet Philip Larkin. The speaker in Larkin's early poem "Toads" envies those carefree souls who don't have to work for a living—who don't have the toad *work* squatting on their lives and soiling "with its sickening poison." He concludes that he

TOAD
Morris Graves
ink and brush drawing
45.8 x 78.5 cm., 1940
Collection, Milwaukee Art Museum

must have a corresponding inner toad that ensures his cowardly acquiescence in the misery of a job. By contrast, the older and wiser speaker in "Toads Revisited," written some years later, takes a closer look at the pathetic jobless, and ends up cheerfully embracing the toad *work*:

> Give me your arm, old toad;
> Help me down Cemetery Road.

Improved human-toad relations are reflected not only in the literature of the past hundred years but also in the realm of folk wisdom, as can be seen in various British and American superstitions: "If a woman has a headache, put a live toad in a piece of white linen and tie it on her head; and she will never have a headache again . . . Tie a live 'hop-toad' on the withers of a horse and it will cure sweeny" [Hyatt: 266, 103]. Old notions about toads and witches playing havoc in the dairy, which undoubtedly meant doom for many a barn-dwelling toad, seem to have been reversed in the proverb "Kill a toad and your cows will give bloody milk" [Randolph 6, 48]. Other dire results of toad murder might be that you will stub your toe, or that your house will catch fire [Hyatt: 71]. Once regarded as poisoners of the drinking water, toads are now coveted as well residents who guarantee the water's purity [Radford and Radford: 240]. The toad even has a romantic role: "A toad crossing the road in front of you indicates that you will see your sweetheart that day" [Hyatt: 327]. "If a toad crosses the path of bridal couple on the way to church, the couple will have prosperity and happiness" [Radford and Radford: 240]. And in the ultrasuperstitious world of American baseball, if a pitcher finds a toad in the outfield before a game, he is sure to win [Hyatt: 433].

THE TOAD AMONG CHILDREN

🐸

*Childhood is a toad in the garden, a
happy toad.*

WILLIAM CARLOS WILLIAMS,
"ROMANCE MODERNE"

In 1904, a reseacher named A.H. Kirkland produced a pamphlet
entitled, "Usefulness of the American Toad" for dissemination by the
U. S. Department of Agriculture. In discussing the toad's enemies,
natural and unatural, he points out that human beings—those who
benefit most from the toad's life—are probably responsible for the
greatest slaughter:

> The heaviest charge of wrongdoing must be entered against
> the small boy, ubiquitous, inquisitive, and often thoughtlessly
> cruel. In a case coming under the writer's notice two boys in
> one afternoon established the disreputable record of 17 dead
> and mutilated toads captured at a breeding pool. Such a
> wanton and expensive exhibition of cruelty may be unique,
> but it is certain that thousands of toads are killed in this way
> annually, and this practice will continue until our boys are
> taught to recognize the value of the toad and to respect its
> rights.   [Kirkland: 14]

The city council of Sefton, England, apparently an active book-banning group, recently yanked Beebee's book on the natterjack from public library shelves, on the ground that the book might inspire children to harm the toad [*Library Journal*, 15 February 1985]. Victor Hugo shows his concern for the same problem in what is probably the best known specimen of French toad poetry, "Le Crapaud," a long and rambling production written around 1858.

The poem's setting is a peaceful country road, with the late afternoon giving a rosy tinge to the clouds and "changing the rain into shimmering droplets." A gentle toad sits by the roadside contemplating the divine when an old priest, lost in his breviary, gratuitously stomps him on the head. Next a beautiful woman with a flower in her blouse drives the point of her umbrella into the toad's eye. But adults can't hold a candle to children when it comes to torturing toads:

The toad was dragging itself along the deeply rutted road.
It was the hour when the fields and lowlands turned sky-blue;
Like a wild beast the toad sought the dark of night; the children saw it
And shouted: "Kill the dreadful thing,
And since it is so vile let's make it suffer!"
And each of them laughing—a child always laughs when he kills something—
Began to stab the toad with pointed sticks,
Enlarging the hole in the gouged-out eye, lacerating
The wound, overjoyed and even applauded by those who passed by;

   ·   ·   ·   ·   ·   ·   ·   ·   ·   ·   ·   ·

It tried to escape; one of its legs had been torn off:
One child began to strike it with a broken shovel;

   ·   ·   ·   ·   ·   ·   ·   ·   ·   ·   ·   ·

Blood was flowing from its forehead; its eye was hanging out;

   ·   ·   ·   ·   ·   ·   ·   ·   ·   ·   ·

Broken, jostled from stone to stone,
It was still breathing, without shelter or sanctuary;
It crawled along; one might think that death, difficult to please,
Found the toad so hideous that he refused to claim it.

                                          trans. Edward Pierce

The toad struggles to a puddle in the ruts of the road, but the children, "with delightful, young and springlike faces," who "had never enjoyed such fun as this," decide to finish it off with a heavy paving stone.

At this point an old donkey appears, lame and weary, pulling a heavy cart, and the boys decide to watch what will happen to the toad under its wheels. But the donkey defies its whip-brandishing driver and lurches painfully out of the miry ruts in order to spare the battered creature:

> *At that moment, dropping the stone from his hand,*
> *One of the children—the same one who is telling this story—*
> *Heard, beneath the infinite and azure celestial arch,*
> *This voice which said to him: "Do always what is right!"*
>
> *[for the entire poem in Pierce's translation, see Appendix B]*

The single sensitive child of Hugo's poem is becoming less of an anomaly in our own time. No doubt there are still children with underdeveloped powers of empathy from whom toads, at once so repulsive and so vulnerable, may continue to receive cruel treatment. But the literature of the last century or so often reflects a more positive relationship between children and toads, as in the following fairy tale:

There was once a little child whose mother gave her every afternoon a small bowl of milk and bread, and the child seated herself in the yard with it. But when she began to eat, a paddock came creeping out of a crevice in the wall, dipped its little head in the dish, and ate with her. The child took pleasure in this, and when she was sitting there with her little dish and the paddock did not come at once, she cried:

> "Paddock, paddock, come swiftly
> Hither come, thou tiny thing,
> Thou shalt have thy crumbs of bread,
> Thou shalt refresh thyself with milk."

Then the paddock came in haste, and enjoyed its food. It even showed gratitude, for it brought the child all kinds of pretty things from its hidden treasures, bright stones, pearls, and golden playthings. The paddock, however, drank only the milk, and left the bread-crumbs alone. Then one day the child took its little spoon and struck the paddock gently on its head, and said: "Eat the bread-crumbs as well, little thing." The mother, who was standing in the kitchen, heard the child talking to someone, and when she saw that she was striking a paddock with her spoon, ran out with a log of wood, and killed the good little creature.

From that time forth, a change came over the child. As long as the paddock had eaten with her, she had grown tall and strong, but now she lost her pretty rosy cheeks and wasted away. It was not long before the funeral bird began to cry in the night, and the redbreast to collect little branches and leaves for a funeral wreath and soon afterwards the child lay on her bier.   [Stern, "Tales of the Paddock," 480–481]

Toads and children seem to share a world that adults neither understand nor approve. This world, as described in the following poem, is no mere childish whimsy, but represents the powerful and positive force of imagination. The inner-demon toad has become an inner angel.

The Little Child's Toad

There was a child
Who met a toad
In a hole in a tree.

"Toad, come with me,"
He said,
"And I will show you the world."

He showed the toad
Buildings, and skyscrapers,
And roller coasters, and movies,

And cookies, and ladies,
And department store hats.
The toad boggled his eyes

To show he was grateful
And let the child ride on his back
While he flew like a carpet.

He gave the child treasures,
And crowns, and jewels,
And finally a princess.

Then the child began to be afraid
He would lose the toad
Who did not sit well with grown-ups:

"Cold, ugly thing," they said.
So he swallowed it.
Then the toad was happier than a toad.

He began to tell the boy
Wonderful tales of the ruby caverns
Pulsing with blood,

And the white islands that float,
And the subways subterranean
In the stomach and blood.

Then the adults began tearing their hair
In fear for love of the toad
The child would turn himself inside out

And never again be seen
In the land.

Susan Fromberg Schaeffer

A great twentieth-century toad boom in children's literature was led by Kenneth Grahame's, *The Wind in the Willows* (1908) and Thornton Burgess's many books, particularly *The Adventures of Old Mr. Toad* (1916). Since then many whimsical tales featuring toad characters, such as those of Arnold Lobel, have been aimed at a growing children's literature market. In many of these works, of course, the toads are not really toads at all but people in animal guise who go sledding, wait anxiously for mail, hunt for missing buttons. A few authors, though, such as Judy Howes in *What I Like About Toads*, Janet Chenery in *The Toad Hunt*, and Lynn Marie Luderer in *The Toad Intruder* do follow

ODE TO A TOAD FROM THE VORCE OF A HORSE

OR "BEING A TOAD AIN'T ALL THAT EASY"

POEM by NANCY WILSON
PICTURES by NANCYOLDS

Get off the road, you crazy toad,
It's obvious you've been boozin'
You crashed into my right front shoe
while I was sorta snoozin'

I've been sniffin' flowers
for hours and hours
awaiting your return
The weeds all grew an
inch or two,
But you showed no
concern

You sent no greetin' to the monthly meetin'
with the Creek Bed Choir Director.
Your last report was much too short
to suit the Toad-Abode Inspector.

You made the scene with the Toad Ball Queen
and squired her 'round the Creek
Doin' lots of drinkin' and not much thinkin',
feelin' super cool and chic.

The 'Toad Quintet hasn't ever met —
there's been no nightly singin'
You forgot to hire a new Toad Choir,
you've been too busy flingin'

Start cruisin' this Creek and fix that leak,
and mend that lilly pad
It'd break my heart- tear me all apart,
to see a fine young toad go bad.

In short, old sport, as a last resort,
you'd better mend your ways
You'll soon be fired, or, perhaps retired-
Fast livin' never pays.

I remember it well, before you raised such hell,
you were a fine young toad
You gotta get back on a proud toad track
and carry your share of the load.

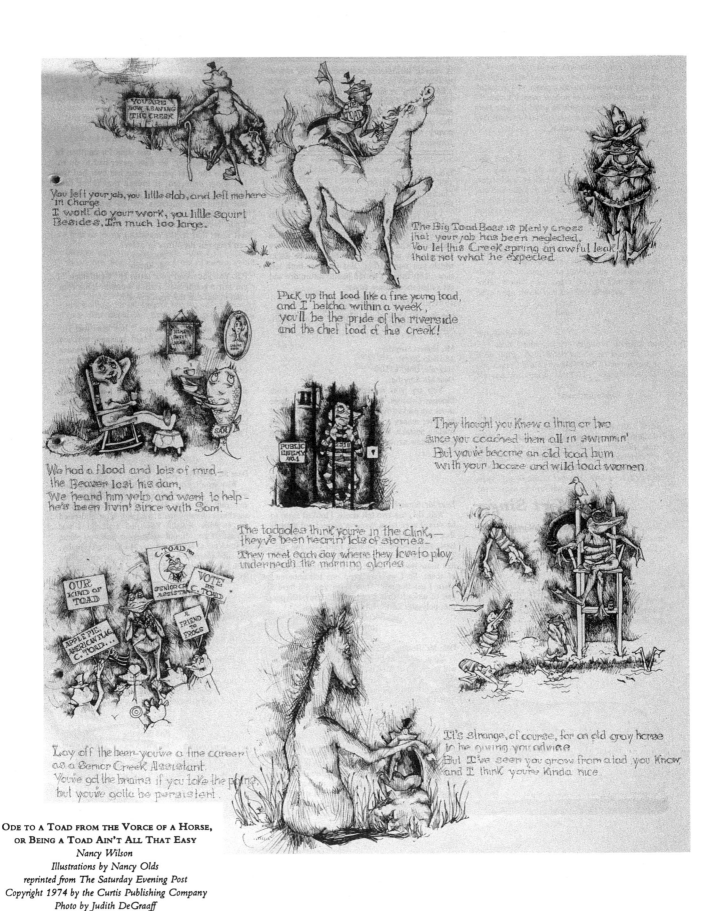

**ODE TO A TOAD FROM THE VORCE OF A HORSE,
OR BEING A TOAD AIN'T ALL THAT EASY**
Nancy Wilson
Illustrations by Nancy Olds
reprinted from The Saturday Evening Post
Copyright 1974 by the Curtis Publishing Company
Photo by Judith DeGraaff

Thornton Burgess in maintaining a certain level of anuran realism—which seems more appropriate for the many grade schoolers who have followed the progress of tadpoles in a classroom aquarium, or watched toadlets in a terrarium at summer camp.

REAL TOADS IN REAL GARDENS

*And mosquitoes inherit the evening while toads no bigger than
    horseflies
Hop crazily after them over the lawns and sidewalks.*

DAVID WAGONER,
"A VALEDICTORY TO STANDARD OIL OF INDIANA"

*But the best thing to do is to set a toad to
catch the bugs. The toad at once establishes
the most intimate relations with the bug. It is
a pleasure to see such unity among the lower
animals.*

CHARLES DUDLEY WARNER,
MY SUMMER IN A GARDEN

No doubt the prevailing modern partiality to toads results partly from the gradual infiltration of scientific thought. In the eighteenth century, the "incomparable" English naturalist Gilbert White was surely unique in demonstrating, in his correspondence, "a respect for all living beings and an almost complete lack of repugnance for toads, spiders and other creatures conventionally thought repulsive" [Thomas, 1983:69]. Some two hundred years later, such Aristotelian objectivity seems to be less rare.

One practical reason for the turn in public opinion is the fact that toads eat bugs. In his pamphlet "Usefulness of the American Toad," Kirkland reports observing toads' feeding habits closely for two years; one summer he actually sliced open 149 toad stomachs and analyzed their contents. Though such a procedure may not be particularly beneficial to the species in the short term, the results obtained were impressive. At least 98 percent of the stomach contents was of animal origin, and of the 93 percent that was identifiable, 77 percent consisted of insects [Kirkland: 8]. Of the toads' total food, 62 percent was made up of harmful insects, though "should ants be included as injurious, as many housekeepers would think proper, this figure would be increased to 81 percent" [Kirkland: 13].

Kirkland found that toads would fill their stomachs to capacity up to four times in a single night, accounting for as many as 55 army worms, 37 tent caterpillars, 65 gypsy moth caterpillars, or 77 thousand-legged worms.

> Mr. F. H. Mosher fed over 30 full-grown celery caterpillars to [a toad] in less than three hours. Doctor Hodge has seen a toad "snap up 86 house flies in less than ten minutes," while he has also published an interesting observation by Ellen M. Foskett, Worcester, Mass., who fed 90 rose bugs to a toad without satisfying its appetite.   [Kirkland: 13]

Kirkland conjectures that in a three-month summer period, a single mature toad might wipe out almost ten thousand noxious insects. Pointing out that some gardeners pay their children a penny for every cutworm destroyed, he ingeniously computes the toad's value on that one item alone at $19.44 [Kirkland: 14].

Later researchers have not always confirmed the ten-thousand-bug total. In one experiment, captive toads were found to average 17 insects per day; in another, toads in the field were found to have eaten about 22 [Heatwole and Heatwole: 697]. Something, of course, depends upon the sizes of toads and insects, but these figures would suggest a three-month toad intake of fifteen hundred to two thousand—which is still a lot of bugs.

And it seems clear that these self-activating natural vacuum cleaners can in fact replace often-dangerous chemical pesticides. Tampering with local fauna is tricky business, and the introduction of *Bufo marinus* into Puerto Rico in 1920, and more recently into Australia, was undoubtedly a mistake. The sugar cane beetles and larvae that the toads were intended to control continue to flourish up in the canes, where they cannot be reached, while the toads have been an ecological disaster. According to a television news report (1990), many inhabitants of Queensland, Australia, are convinced that the proliferating giant toads, having no natural enemies, will soon form a living carpet over much of their state. Still, there must be ways in which, without disturbing nature's balance, indigenous toads could be more effectively used in controlling insects. No one, for example, seems yet to have followed up on the suggestion that spadefoot tadpoles' appetite for mosquito larvae might be useful [Barber and King: 3190]. But at least one U.S. country club sponsors a children's movie matinee with one live toad as the price of admission; apparently the toads keep down the slugs and mole crickets that afflict the greens [Wainio: 20]. And for those who don't regard the cure as worse than the disease, Allan Wainio suggests something even closer to home:

> Are you having trouble with cockroaches in the kitchen? Well, don't run to the nearest hardware store for the latest cockroach poison. Take a stroll by some pond or stream, catch a chubby little toad, and bring him home. Toads just love lapping up those cockroaches. Lock the toad in the kitchen for a few nights, and your cockroach problems are over. By then, you will have the fattest toad in town.   [Wainio: 20]

Domestic arrangements like these can lead to warm toad relations. Dorothy Long's toad, a robust *Bufo americanus* named Winstonia, when not in residence in Long's bathtub or victory garden, became a legend in the Carnegie Museum herpetology laboratory for feats of ingestion—152 Mexican bean beetles within an hour, one cherry tomato rolling across the floor, one large and very poisonous black widow spider. Long calculated a summer's supply of small insects for Winstonia at 22,700 [Long: 212–213].

Mary Bowling, who recommends that every gardener "cultivate [the] little amphibian's acquaintance," finds these bug hunters very responsive to the "soft touch":

> Once accustomed to gentle handling, a toad will settle serenely in your open palm, often stretching out one hind leg at a time to have it stroked and scratched.   [Bowling: 72]

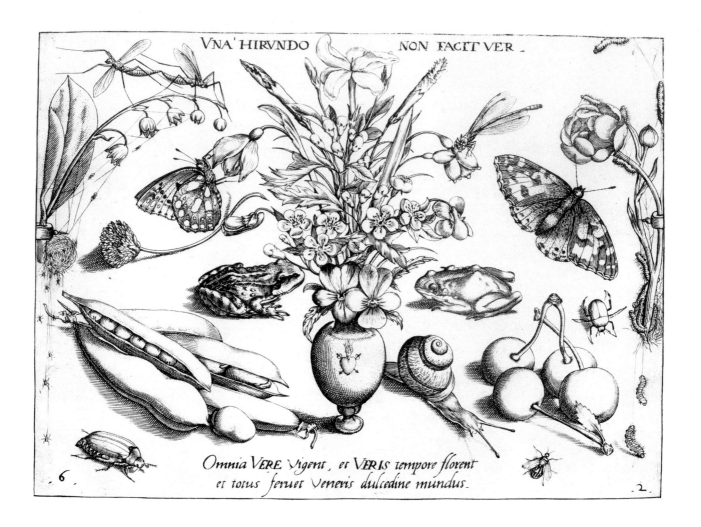

UNA HIRVNDO   NON FACIT VER

Omnia VERE vigent, et VERIS tempore florent
et totus feruet Veneris dulcedine mundus.

The Latin may be translated: One Swallow does not make a Spring. In the Spring all things are invigorated and blossom, and the whole world burns sweetly with the pleasures of love.

Most people seem content to leave the toads outside. The gopher holes in D. R. Wallace's garden formed lovely burrows for a number of large toads. Fascinated by them, Wallace would "go out at night with a flashlight and see what appeared to be a pair of black eyes sparkling solemnly from the earth itself—as though my garden had grown sense organs." Twilight watering would bring out "a dignified toad that I half expected to be carrying a towel and bar of soap, ready for its daily shower" [Wallace: 68].

UNA HIRUNDO
*Jakob Hoefnagel
(after George Hoefnagel)
engraving, 1592
Philadelphia Museum of Art,
58-19-20
Given by Lessing J. Rosenwald
Photo by Philadelphia
Museum of Art*

Shoveling a Toad

Tossing garden dirt,
I am suddenly surprised—
check the next shovelful.
I have heaved up a toad,
who sits unmoving on the dirt
in the blue wheelbarrow.
He is beautiful,
so fat his legs seem an afterthought.
The dirt has fallen away cleanly,
leaving all his knobs and whorls knurled
and mottled in the late sunlight.
He is still in his winter sleep,
puzzled, eventually blinking.
As I pick him up and move him off
to a quiet place under the rhubarb,
he surges and struggles a little.
He is soft as an old tomato.

Paul O. Williams

Many toad-loving gardeners furnish blueprints for better toadhomes in gardens. These should be underground, in order to remain cool and damp through the heat of summer days. The simplest construction is an earthenware flower pot with an entrance broken into one side, buried upside down an inch or two below ground, with a small tunnel excavated to the doorway. Flower pots should be small, since toads like to feel the walls on all sides. They will remain coolest if shaded, and with the entrance facing north, but they should not be placed in low points where the runoff from every shower of rain will cause major flooding.

Toad in a Flower Pot

A toad slumped in a flower pot
settled himself at home
among the sprouting seeds,
a little square pot
he filled with his
soft bulk

like a cat
curled in a coal scuttle.
The disarranged geometry
of his brown spots
wrinkled over his flowing mass,
a torpid clod
fitted to corners,
his slow eye
with its golden slit
watching.

      Nancy Culbertson

THE HONEY SISTERS
DOING A GARDEN BLESSING
David James Gilhooly, III
Photo by David James Gilhooly, III

THE TOAD TODAY

What, where or how, appreciate those who tell
How the toad lives: it lives—enough for me!

ROBERT BROWNING

The Carolina toad, wrote John Edwards Holbrook in the last century, "is timid and remarkably gentle in its habits":

> I have seen an individual kept for a long space of time, which became perfectly tame: during the summer months he would retire to a corner of the room, into a habitation he had prepared for himself, in a small quantity of earth, placed there for his convenience.... Some water having been squeezed from a sponge upon his head one hot day in July, he returned the next to the same spot, and seemed very well pleased with the repetition; nor did he fail during the extreme heat of the summer to repair to it frequently, in search of his shower-bath. [Holbrook: 9–10]

Human-toad congeniality in our day is no longer monopolized by either hags or herpetologists. Lifelong love affairs with toads, like that of Terence Shortt, the dean of Canadian bird painters, are ever more common. Mr. Shortt communed with toads under the veranda as a boy, sneaking the porch light on after the grownups had gone to bed in order to procure snacks of dazed insects for his midnight guests [Shortt: 25-26]. The marvelous watercolors that he later produced of toads from around the world surely establish Mr. Shortt as the premier toad painter of the Western world (see illustrations on pages xv, 33, 67, 184).

A Toad Sketched in Ballpoint

A mile and a half up from Lena Lake,
Where the trail came down close to the main creek,
I saw a big fat boreal-toad walking
toward me just before it saw me and froze.

As I sketched its contours in ballpoint,
I liked its pose more and more, arms around
a pebble, pale throat bubbling away,
yellow eyes with bar-shaped pupils watching.

I wanted that cool fatness in my hands,
to feel its strength, to see it more closely,
but before I disturbed it, I needed
to finish scribbling its blotchy markings.

The toad on my paper was not the toad;
yet it had a toadishness of its own
which filled my need. When I walked up the path
and the toad was hopping, I did not grab it.

Carl Miller

Actually handling the hopping toads has proven to be a practical way of preventing the massive springtime slaughter of toads upon highways. Some years ago one Norman Gammon, disturbed by the number of toad corpses on a lovers' lane near London, organized twenty-five neighbors who, with flashlights and buckets, transported some twelve hundred toads to their nearby mating pond, thereby ensuring that both human and toad rendezvous could proceed on schedule [Montgomery: 70]. Throughout Western Europe, such toad patrols have now become common.

Officials in West Germany, Holland, and Switzerland also sponsor international "toad-crossing" conferences to spread

the word about the latest techniques for helping toads migrate. What's more, in many parts of West Germany road signs now warn motorists to "Beware of Toad Traffic."

Authorities hope such efforts will help turn around declining toad populations.

["Escorting Toads Across Highways": 28]

The Toad

I carelessly flick a bug away.
To Hell with it. A wasp I'd respect.

There was the time, though, that I helped
the little old toad across Concord Avenue.
I was walking home. The toad hopped
in front of me out into the late
light traffic. Well, I said to myself,
What's one less toad in the world?
Worse cataclysms threaten . . .

                A tire
whizzed and missed him. He had made his
(or her) slow, hesitant way almost
to the vast middle of the westbound side.
If he hopped like mad, he had a chance . . .
He didn't even understand the problem.
I found a stick, walked out, prodded.
I never thought of picking him up.
It was his project. It wasn't mine.

We made it to the center island.
But there he couldn't hop high enough
to get himself up onto the curb,
so I had to keep on prodding him
further on, to a break in the island,
then on further, across the eastbound lanes,
then on, yet again, to a curb break
on the far side. He kept getting tired
and giving up. What was this strange
stick, this suffering decreed?

                Me?
I wanted to get home. I had no need . . .
no fear . . . and weren't we a sight!
Two busybodies, touching, in the night.

                        Richard Moore

The latest British strategy has been the construction of toad passageways beneath busy highways. But perhaps the most significant measure of modern *Bufo* sympathy is the fact that several species of toads are now officially on the "endangered" list—though some may need even more help than that to survive. *Bufo houstonensis*, for instance, competing directly as it does with the city of Houston for living space, doesn't seem to have much of a chance. The odds on the very rare crested toad of Puerto Rico may be much better, thanks to the efforts of Rick Paine, who succeeded in breeding them (with the aid of "hormonal inducements") at the Buffalo Zoo and recently returned five hundred of them to their homeland. If they can find a niche or two not filled by imported *Bufo marinus*, possibly among the eroded limestone formations they love so well, they may make it yet.

If the tide of human emotion has really shifted in favor of full-hearted toad support, the time may at last be ripe for an idea first offered to science by the eccentric eighteenth-century English physician John Hill:

PUERTO RICAN CRESTED
TOAD
Peltophryne lemur
Photo by Sheila D. Lanz,
courtesy of the Buffalo Zoo

> BUFO is a constellation offered to the astronomical world, and composed of a number of unformed stars near the sign Libra.
> The animal is the common toad, mentioned by all the

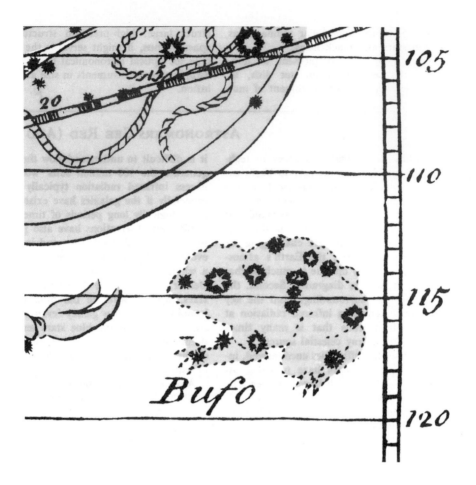

writers on natural history, and celebrated among the vulgar, to a proverb, for the brightness of its eyes.

It is but a small asterism, but for the space which it occupies in the heavens, it contains a very fair portion of stars; these have always been considered as a conspicuous cluster, and it is wonderful that they have not before been arranged under the form of some animal.

The conspicuous stars in the constellation Bufo are fifteen and some of them are remarkably bright and considerable; in the head there are only two, one is near the extremity or mouth, and this is a small one; the other, which may be called the Toad's Eye, is a very fine one of second magnitude.

[cited in Drennan: 316]

Surely by now *Bufo* has earned his apotheosis among the stars.

BUFO
The Constellation from A New Astronomical Dictionary *John Hill*
1768
reprinted from Anthony Drennan, Sky and Telescope *65 (April, 1983): 316*

APPENDIX A

The Great Toad Hunt

Good friends of ours had built a place out in the country and had worked hard all summer on the courtyard. My wife and I often drove out in the afternoons to help them, for we live in a small apartment and otherwise have little chance to spend time out of doors. We helped spread the fill that was trucked in; we brought up from the river smooth stones whose sheen broke strongly from the absorptive texture of the foliage; we carried flagstone, and padded it into place with sand. Our friends were old and dear and much of the work was done in silence with the usual line between host and guest submerged in a common concern for the beauty of stone and plant. I believe we all had the desire to create in this courtyard a place of rich associations, so that individual rocks and plants could be linked to particular events and individual emotions. We wished, I believe, to be able to point to almost anything in the courtyard and say: "Do you remember . . ." And we could all smile and nod our heads, and laugh, perhaps. Certain stones, for example, have affinities for each other that can only be discovered by accident.

The courtyard added to its store of memories each day, and before half the summer had passed other lives had given their assent and benediction to it as well. There were always the impermanent birds, billowing with energy, impatient with time: There were the small insects that could, if necessary, be killed: sow bugs, ants, earthworms, and simple-minded flying things that annoyed: and there were those that must never be killed: moths, butterflies, harvestmen and spiders. But most especially there was one spider, a humped orb weaver, *Aranea gemmoides*, that lived high and secure in the eaves like a watchman on the Cornish cliffs. She was wholly immune to time, for she had not arrived until full grown and when fall came she would not so much die as disappear. I never saw her leave the small

hiding place she had fashioned behind her trap web, and I never saw her catch anything.

One afternoon we sat, feet pressed against the warm flagstones, and talked of the life that had already come to the new courtyard, and as I looked at the small rose drops of wine on the stone, my wife first mentioned the suitability of the toad to such surroundings. "The spider is just for the summer," she said, her voice coming from the shade, "and a toad lives many, many years."

I proposed a toast with enthusiasm, which was not unusual, and we began to chat about toads. They are, I declared, natural wits, and to include toad in our conversations, to ask his advice, and to seek his company in the early morning would be experiences reminiscent of certain Chinese poets.

Someone went into the house for a toad book and after a few minutes' consultation it was obvious that *Bufo boreas boreas,* Baird's Toad, was the most likely, as it could be found locally. And this might make the difference between possession and desire. For we agreed that a toad is not to be *bought.* Initially there is the difficulty of finding someone with a toad to sell, and secondly there is some

HIMALAYAN GREEN TOAD
BUFO VIRIDIS
Terence Shortt
watercolor and graphite on paper
19.6 x 27.9 cm., 1963
Collection of Martina R. Norelli
Photo by Gene Young

arcane principle at work that states that toads ought to be *found*. It is best that one appear spontaneously in the garden, as do mushrooms and visiting orioles, but it is permissible to make an active quest for one, going into the forest, croaking impassionedly, and turning stones. To wait for the spontaneous generation of a toad in this particular courtyard seemed excessive, and we decided a hunt must be made.

The forest which was available to us had no name. It could not be called Arden, Birnam, Westermain, or even Black. It was merely the forest. And yet it was not, for I had once calculated that it was possible to cross no more than five paved roads and travel from our forest to the North Pole. It was as if it had such depths that we could point to a spot and say that *that* was where Lear's Fool left earth. Certainly we should find a toad.

We decided that the morning sun, some bottles of Sauterne, sour French bread, a salad dosed with herbs and kept cold by ice, some rotty-looking cheese, and a pail of onion soup would keep us from collapsing on the trail. We would arise deliberately early, climb into one car, and aim ourselves at the nearest toad. My wife remarked as we left for our apartment that she hoped it would not take too long to locate a sympathetic toad. "For," she reminded us, "he must assent to it all."

We did not understand what she meant, but it seemed a nice conceit, and we agreed: any toad that struggled was to be released.

The road had taken a mountain and held it up with loose loops, cradling it as a promontory, an inverted bowl, sustaining its height. The apex of the mound was indented slightly, and a meadow appeared, rich in wild legumes, and where the water came, bunch grass thickets. The road lapsed into a single string of dirt, pitted with the marks of deer. Their sharp hooves had crushed even the roots of grass and nothing grew. We stopped the car and for a moment sat without moving. The silence came at us and we watched the seed-heavy tops of the grass wave noiselessly. Down by the stream cow parsnip raised its seeds in banks of angry fists, like revolutionists. There were no blossoms anywhere, just seeds.

The wind was from the west, and it caught my wife's hair as she climbed from the car and lifted it from her shoulders. For one quick moment it rested in the air like the hair of Botticelli's Venus. She laughed, and shook it once and put her scarf on. She extended her hand to help me from the car (my leg has been bad since North Africa), and we stood together looking across the bowl to the far forest rim where one group of Douglas fir stood higher than the rest.

"We should all separate," my wife said, "for there's no rime or reason to toads. Be nosy, look under everything, and watch for movement in the grass." Our friends, knowing our ways, nodded and proceeded according to their own theories. I decided to head towards the tall stand of fir. My wife walked to the stream and indicated that she would follow it.

Grass held the majority in that meadow, but every few steps there would be a ghetto of small plants thriving in the crowded ground. The first I saw, on my left, was a sturdy growth of false asphodel, a poisonous lily. There was some larkspur a few paces on, and it became a method of measuring distance to note only the poisonous plants. Steers-head, silvery lupine, dog-bane, and mixed with the cow parsley along the stream, water hemlock. I was strangely elated with the presence of these plants, but simultaneously countered the effect in my mind with a warning not to be morbid. There was life in the meadow as well. Low on the ground were the sheet webs of the grass spiders, and it seemed civilized insolence to be able to remember that a hundred years ago the Burgmans of Innsbruck painted on this silk.

At times the grass rose to my waist, but ordinarily it was knee-high and thickly bunched. I watched carefully for signs of movement contrary to that caused by the wind, and twice I thought I saw a movement, generated at the ground, swing the tops and mark the passage of a toad. I was twice mistaken: once by an eddying current of wind, and once by a small green snake that hurried out of my vision in a panic. As I remembered, the movement had been too sinuous for that of a toad; what I should watch for was a lumpy gait, a ruminative hopping that would cause the grass to twitch.

Halfway to the tall firs I saw it: the uneven pulsing of the grass that was the mark of toad on a mid-morning stroll. After a moment's unhappy and thrashing attempt at stealth, I decided that speed was my forte, and I began to trot towards the advancing movement in the grass. With greater skill than I knew I possessed, I reached the spot, stooped down, and plucked from the grass a sweet-smelling toad. That was the first quality I sensed: the toad smelled good.

I had clapped my hands together to hold it, and for a moment I could not see it. Then I carefully made a window with my thumbs and looked inside. An emerald-green toad with ruby eyes looked out at me. There was a diamond set square in his forehead.

If my reflexes had been at all quick, I am sure I would have dropped the toad and sprinted for sanity, but my synapses are in such poor condition that before I could react, I had realized the significance of what I held.

"Do I kiss you, or rub you like a lamp?" I asked, certain I had a prince of some realm safe in my hands. The toad made no answer and as I watched its constant eyes, I thought how obtuse most characters in fairy stories are. It takes them months and years to realize that the pink lamb is somebody's sister. It had taken me ten seconds to turn my twentieth-century heritage of rationalism upside down and begin to think in terms of magic and enchantment. I could easily imagine an empirically-minded gentleman reaching for his penknife and working on the diamond.

These moments of fantasy were brief. I noticed that the toad had not struggled, and therefore was fair game, and gave the diamond a small, sharp tap with my fingernail. The toad blinked, but there was a brittle quality to the sound that served to corroborate my eyes. I stroked his head and shoulders with two fingers and repeated "Kubla Khan" and the first lines of "Tyger, tyger, burning bright," but these did no good. Then I kissed him, but nothing happened. I walked back to the car.

I returned by a different route than that which had led to the toad, and I carried the rich-green squatting one in my hands as though he were some rare and medicinal wine being hurried to a dying king. Had I photographed the scene I should have focused on the contrast between my legs' brash and jolting progress and the brittle, slender quiet of the bunch grass, then quickly faded to a close-up of my face, lean-cheeked, hawk-nosed, staring ahead, and in the distance, firs that might have grown in Lapland.

We had carefully provided ourselves with a small cardboard box for captive toad, and I was able to place him there with no trouble. I even put a handful of crushed grass on the bottom for his comfort. He sat quite still, eyes blood deep and hushed, only the small sac at his throat pulsating as he breathed. I put the box down in the shade of the car and drew one of the sauterne bottles from the picnic basket. Triumph required a toast, even if solitary. A gesture for toad with the glass, a moment's hesitating gaze at the rim of trees through the lucid wine, and I was celebrating. In half an hour or so our friends returned from their quest, unfulfilled. I saw Jonas first, whistling and swinging a stick. Madelaine came later, three interesting rocks in her hands pulling her shoulders down.

I had decided to keep my magic toad a secret until my wife returned, for more than any of us she would understand what to do. Whatever she decided, I thought, we must decide too. I poured a glass of wine for Jonas and we stood by the hood of the car, watching Madelaine approach.

"Those are good rocks," Jonas said, and Madelaine smiled and nodded as she dropped them to the ground.

We sat together in the shade of the car and I handed Madelaine a glass of wine.

"I'm starved," she said, taking the glass from my hand. "I wonder if Wing would mind if I ate a piece of her bread?"

I rummaged in the picnic basket and brought out the loaf. We cut a few pieces and crumbled some cheese onto them, and then once more leaned against the car, staring at the far rim of trees. The tranquility was like that of the courtyard. No one spoke, but there was relief at each other's presence, as though the body warmth, even the small node of gravitational force that the mass of each of our bodies possessed was felt. This interior transmission of presence, this unspoken colloquy, was only gently displaced by my wife's shout from the stream.

She waved, and we looked up, and then she was among us. "It was like holding a fool's fire," she said. "A tourmaline toad as acrobatic as the wind. Well, we know he didn't agree to come along and live in the courtyard." Her face was happy and she wiped her hands on her slacks before she took the glass of wine I held out. She made the gesture and took a swallow. "Comfort me with flagons and stay me with salads, for I am sick of toads." There was a charming and deliberately wry smile on her face.

We all sat down once more and I put the picnic basket in front of us and poured cups of soup from the vacuum bottle. We chattered aimlessly while we ate, and I watched carefully to see that every one had plenty. Jonas and Madelaine had not even seen a toad, and Wing had lost hers and I waited until we had finished eating before telling them of my discovery. I remember sitting crosslegged, holding the small cardboard box and recounting in some detail the progress of my quest: the poisonous plants seriatim, the stalk, the rush, the dolorous blow, and the astonishment. They sat quite still, absorbing the idea.

Looking directly into my wife's eyes, I said, "I have kissed it and rubbed it like a lamp, Wing, and nothing has happened," and I opened the box. "Perhaps you will know how to heal the spell, if healing is what it needs." I handed the toad to Wing and she held it in her hands as though it were a small bird. Jonas and Madelaine strained towards her to see.

"Why, it's a perfectly lovely diamond," Wing said. "I don't know that we'll have to do anything at all about the spell. Toad seems so very content." She widened the cup of her hands and raised them slightly in a gesture of offering. The toad sat still in her hands and the rest of us watched as he blinked, and then settled into her palms.

Madelaine, sitting next to me, brushed my hand with her fingers and kissed me lightly on the cheek. "I think Wing is right, Sam. Toad seems happy and we might never find out how to break the spell."

Howard McCord

Appendix B

Le Crapaud (The Toad)

How little man really understands of life's mysteries!
The setting sun was shining through rose colored clouds;
The incident happened towards the end of a day of storms, while the
Setting sun was changing the rain into shimmering droplets;
Close by a road, at the edge of a rain-filled pool,
There sat a toad, staring with amazement towards the sky;
The toad's manner was solemn and dreamlike; the horrible contemplating the divine.
(Oh who can explain the existence of suffering and ugliness?
The world is full of petty emperors and
Unscrupulous rulers just as toads are covered with warts
And meadows are filled with flowers and the skies with sunlight!)
The water in the road appeared to shimmer through the grass;
Evening was unfolding like a banner;
A bird lowered its song as the day's light grew dim;
The wind and streams grew calm; and without a care,
Without a fear, without shame or anger,
The gentle toad looked up at the sun's halo;
Perhaps this cursed creature felt touched by grace,
Since there exists not a single living creature who does not reflect the infinite;
There exists no soul so base and abject as not to be touched
By the light from above, which can be tender or fierce;
There exists no wretched creature, however pitiful, impure or vile,
Who does not reflect the immensity of the universe in his eyes.
A man who was passing by saw the hideous creature,
And shuddering, stepped on its head with his heel;
The man happened to be a priest who was reading his breviary;
Then came a woman wearing a flower in her blouse,

And she drove the point of her umbrella into the toad's eye;
The priest was rather old and the woman was quite beautiful.

Then came four schoolboys without a care in the world.
I was once a child, young and cruel;
Every man on earth, where the soul wanders in slavery,
Can thus begin the story of his life.
A child's face speaks of play, of joy and of hope;
Children have loving mothers and live happily,
Joyful young men breathing in the air,
Filling their lungs, cherished, carefree and happy; what more
Might they require unless it be to torture some unfortunate beast?
The toad was dragging itself along the deeply rutted road.
It was the hour when the fields and lowlands turned sky-blue;
Like a wild beast the toad sought the dark of night; the children saw it
And shouted: "Kill the dreadful thing,
And since it is so vile let's make it suffer!"
And each of them laughing—a child always laughs when he kills something—
Began to stab the toad with pointed sticks,
Enlarging the hole in the gouged-out eye, lacerating
The wound, overjoyed, and even applauded by those who passed by;
And those who passed by also began laughing; and a sinister cloud
Descended on the black martyr who could not even sound a death rattle,
Terrible blood flowed from every part of the body
Of this poor creature whose only wrong was to be ugly;
It tried to escape; one of its legs had been torn off;
One child began to strike it with a broken shovel;
Each blow brought foam to the mouth of the prisoner,
Who even on bright sunfilled days had to crawl at the bottom of some cave;
The children shouted: "How evil it is! it's drooling!"
Blood was flowing from its forehead; its eye was hanging out;
Horrible to look at, it made its way through the brambles and gennet;
One would have thought it came from a greenhouse of horrors!
This terrible act made its misery worse!
Adding horror to its deformity!
Broken, jostled from stone to stone,
It was still breathing, without shelter or sanctuary;
It crawled along; one might think that death, difficult to please,
Found the toad so hideous that he refused to claim it.

The children tried to seize the toad with a snare,
But it eluded them by slipping into a hedgerow;
The tracks in the road were quite deep and the toad dragged itself to them
And plunged in, broken, bleeding, its skull split open,
Feeling a little freshness in the greenish water,
Washing itself of man's cruelty in the mud;
The children with delightful, young and springlike
Faces had never enjoyed such fun as this;

They were all talking at once and the elders shouted
To the younger: "Come look at it! Say, Adolphe and Pierre,
Let's find a big rock and finish it off!"
All as one they fixed their stares
On this horrible creature and it desperately
Watched those terrible eyes looking down at it.
Alas! Man needs goals, but why must they include victims;
Whenever man acts at any point along the human horizon,
Let his hand bear life instead of death.
All eyes followed the toad as it moved through the slime;
The faces were full of both rage and ecstasy;
One of the children returned carrying a paving stone;
The stone was very heavy, but the evil intention made it light to carry;
The child said: "Now we are going to see what this can do."
Now at this very moment and place,
Chance had it that a heavily loaded wagon passed by,
Pulled by a lame old donkey who was scrawny and deaf;
The old donkey, limping and pathetic to see,
Was returning to the stable after a day of work;
It pulled the wagon and carried a large basket upon its back;
Each step appeared to be its last;
The beast trudged along, weary and beaten;
The whip cracked around it in a storm of blows;
One could see in the donkey's watery and clouded eyes
A look of stupidity, which was perhaps just stupor;
The wheel ruts were so deep and full of mud
And of such a steep angle that each turn of the wheel
Was like a deadly painful wrenching;
The donkey went forward moaning as the driver cursed it;
The road entered an incline and the donkey went a little faster;
It was dreaming passively beneath the blows of the whip and cudgel
In a deep trance-like state where men never venture.

The children, upon hearing the turning wheels and treading hooves,
Turned around, saw the approaching cart and shouted:
"Stop! Don't crush the toad with the stone!
Look, a cart is coming down the hill
And is going to run over the toad and that is even better."
They all stood watching.

Suddenly, while advancing in the wheel ruts
Where the victim was waiting its final torture,
The donkey saw the toad and, sadly bending down over
A creature who was, alas, even sadder than itself, weighed down, broken, dejected,
    skinned,
The donkey lowered its head and seemed for a moment to sense the situation;
This slave, this condemned prisoner, so patient, showed mercy;
It summoned all its ebbing strength and stiffened against

The chain and harness until blood flowed from its muscles,
And fought the driver who raged at it to move on.
Surmounting the terrible gravity of its burden,
Accepting the struggle despite its exhaustion,
It dragged along the cart and forced the packsaddle upward,
And though weary still managed to turn the unwilling wheel,
Leaving behind the miserable toad to live a little longer;
Then under the crack of the whip the donkey continued on its way.

At that moment, dropping the stone from his hand,
One of the children—the same one who is telling this story—
Heard beneath the infinite and azure celestial arch,
This voice which said to him: "Do always what is right!"

The virtue of a mindless creature! like a diamond made from coal;
Heavenly mystery! Noble light that springs from the darkness!
Heavenly creatures possess no more virtue than pathetic ones,
When the pathetic, the blind and tortured,
Reflect and, even though they are without joy, can show mercy.
O sacred spectacle! The lowly coming to the rescue of the lowly,
The obscure creature coming to the aid of the disheartened one,
A dumb beast tenderly leans over to help a hideous one;
The virtue of the damned should cause the chosen to reflect!
An animal steps forward to help what man considers repulsive!
In the calm of a pale sunset
There are times when the beast thinks that it is related
To the mysterious gentleness of existence;
All that is needed is a flash of grace to fall upon it
For it to become equal to the eternal stars;
A donkey returning home one night, overworked and exhausted,
Near its end, despite the pain in its blood-spattered hooves,
Takes a few extra steps and goes out of its way to avoid
Crushing a toad in the mire;
That donkey, downtrodden, uncared for, and abused by the whip,
Has more virtue than Socrates and more grandeur than Plato.
Are you, a philosopher, seeking the truth? Are you, a thinker, contemplating reality?
Would you like to find the truth concealed here in man's cursed darkness?
Trust, cry out, and drown yourself in unfathomable love!
Whoever is good will find the truth concealed in darkness;
Whoever is good carries within himself a part of paradise. Oh Sage,
Goodness, which lights up the face of the world,
Goodness, seen in guileless hope,
Goodness, a pure ray of light which gives warmth to the unknown,
An instinct which amid darkness and suffering can love,
This is the ineffable and supreme union
That brings together, alas! so often in misfortune,
An ignorant beast, a donkey, with the all-knowing God.

Victor Hugo (trans. by Edward Pierce)

BIBLIOGRAPHY

Abel, J. J., and Macht, D. I. 1911. "The poisons of the tropical toad, *Bufo agua*." *Journal of the American Medical Association* 56: 1531–1536.

Abel-Vidor, Suzanne, et al. 1981. *Between Continents/Between Seas: Precolumbian Art of Costa Rica.*. New York: Harry N. Abrams.

"Acquisitions: Two North American Indian Wood Carvings." 1976. *St. Louis City Art Museum Bulletin* 12 (1): 1–6.

Adler, Doris. 1981. "Imaginary Toads in Real Gardens." *English Literary Renaissance* 11 (3): 235–260.

Alexander, T. R. 1964. "Observations on the Feeding Behavior of *Bufo marinus* (Linne)." *Herpetologica* 20 (4): 255–259.

Allen, A. 1979. "Toads: The Biochemistry of the Witches' Cauldron." *History Today* 29 (April): 265–268.

Altig, R. 1979. *Toads Are Nice People*. Eldon, Mo.: Manco.

Awbrey, F. T. 1963. "Homing and Home Range in *Bufo valliceps*." *Texas Journal of Science* 15: 135–141.

Bajger, J. 1980. "Diversity of Defensive Responses in Populations of Fire Toads (*Bombina bombina* and *Bombina variegata*)." *Herpetologica* 36 (2): 133–137.

Barber, M. A., and King, C. H. 1927. "The Tadpole of the Spadefoot Toad: An Enemy of Mosquito Larvae." *U.S. Public Health Service: Public Health Reports* 42 (No. 52): 3189–3193.

Baskin, W. 1972. *Dictionary of Satanism*. London: Peter Owen.

Bates, Scott. 1983. "The Perfect Toad." In *Lupo's Fables*. Sewanee, Tenn.: Jump-Off Mountain Press.

Bax, D. 1979. *Hieronymus Bosch: His Picture-Writing Deciphered*. Rotterdam: A. A. Balkema.

Beebee, T. J. C. 1983. *The Natterjack Toad*. London: Oxford University Press.

Behler, J. L., and King, F. W. 1979. *The Audubon Society Field Guide to North American Reptiles and Amphibians*. New York: Alfred A. Knopf.

Belt, S. C. 1975. "Frogs and Toads in Oriental Art and Myth." *Terra* 14 (4): 39–42.

Bennett, A. F. 1980. "The Metabolic Foundations of Vertebrate Behavior." *BioScience* 30: 452–456.

Benson, A. C. 1909. "The Toad." In *The Poems of A. C. Benson*. New York: John Lane.

Benson, E. P., ed. 1981. *The Olmec and Their Neighbors: Essays in Memory of Matthew W. Stirling*. Washington, D.C.: Dumbarton Oaks.

Bernal, I. 1969. *The Olmec World*. Translated by D. Heyden and F. Horcasitas. Berkeley and Los Angeles: University of California Press.

Bernal, I., et al. 1973. *The Iconography of Middle American Sculpture*. New York: Metropolitan Museum of Art.

Bettelheim, Bruno. 1976. *The Uses of Enchantment: The Meaning and Importance of Fairy Tales*. New York: Alfred A. Knopf.

Bierce, Ambrose. 1946. *The Collected Writings of Ambrose Bierce*. Edited by C. Fadiman. New York: Citadel Press.

Bishop, Elizabeth. 1983. *The Complete Poems, 1927–1979*. New York: Farrar, Straus and Giroux.

Blair, W. F., ed. 1972. *Evolution in the Genus Bufo*. Austin: University of Texas Press.

———. 1974. "Character Displacement in Frogs." *American Zoology* 14: 1119–1125.

Bogert, C. M. 1947. "Results of the Archbold Expeditions, No. 57: A Field Study of Homing in the Carolina Toad." *American Museum Novitates* 1355: 1–24.

———. 1954. "Amphibians, Pioneers on Land," pp. 1191–1193. "The Frogs and Toads—Amphibians without Tails," pp. 1218–1238. In *The Animal Kingdom* ed. F. Drimmer. New York: Doubleday and Co..

Boice, R. 1970. "Avoidance Learning in Active and Passive Frogs and Toads." *Journal of Comparative and Physiological Psychology* 70: 154–156.

Bowling, M. B. 1983. "Get Yourself a Toad!" *Mother Earth News* (July–August): 72.

Boys, F., and Smith, H. M. 1959. *Poisonous Amphibians and Reptiles: Recognition and Bite Treatment*. Springfield, Ill.: Charles C. Thomas.

Bragg, A. N. 1957. "Some Factors in the Feeding of Toads." *Herpetologica* 13: 189–191.

———. 1965. *Gnomes of the Night: The Spadefoot Toads*. Philadelphia: University of Pennsylvania Press.

Brandon, E. 1976. "Folk Medicine in French Louisiana" In *American Folk Medicine: A Symposium*, ed. W. D. Hand, pp. 215–234. Berkeley and Los Angeles: University of California Press.

"British Book Banning: Medicine, Huxley, and Toads." 1985. *Library Journal* 110 (3): 95.

Broad, W., and Wade, N. 1982. *Betrayers of the Truth*. New York: Simon and Schuster.

Brower, L. P., and Brower, J. V. Z. 1962. "Investigations into Mimicry." *Natural History* 71: 8–19.

Brown, H. A. 1976. "The Status of California and Arizona Populations of the Western Spadefoot Toads (genus *Scaphiopus*)." *Contributions in Science* 286: 1–15.

Browne, Sir Thomas. 1862. *Religio Medici*. Boston: Ticknor and Fields.

Browning, Robert. 1895. *The Complete Poetic and Dramatic Works of Robert Browning*. Edited by Horace E. Scudder. New York: Houghton Mifflin.

Budge, E. A. W. 1913. *The Syriac Book of Medicines*, I and II. London: Oxford University Press. Reprint 1976. Amsterdam: Philo Press.

"Buffalo Zoo is Love-nest for Rare Toads." 29 April 1984. *Syracuse Herald American*: A-6.

Bunyan, John. 1965. *The Pilgrim's Progress*. Edited by R. Sharrock. New York: Penguin Books.

Burgess, Thornton W. 1916. *The Adventures of Old Mr. Toad*. New York: Grosset and Dunlap.

Burland, C. 1968. *North American Indian Mythology*. London: Paul Hamlyn.

Burroughs, John. 1906. "The Song of the Toad." In *Bird and Bough*. Boston: Houghton Mifflin.

Busack, S. D., and Bury, R. B. 1975. "Toad in Exile." *National Parks and Conservation* 49 (March): 15–16.

Bushnell, G. H. S. 1965. *Ancient Arts of the Americas*. New York: Praeger.

Cannon, M. S. 1973. "Beautiful, Bold and Venomous." *Smithsonian* 4 (2): 53–57.

Carroll, Lewis. 1934. *The Lewis Carroll Book* (Edited by Richard Herrick). New York: Dial Press.

Carroll, P, ed. 1968. *The Young American Poets*. New York: Follett.

Cauthen, I. B. 1973. "Satan 'squat like a toad.' " *Milton Quarterly* 7: 95–97.

Chambers, A. B. 1967. "Three Notes on Eve's Dream in *Paradise Lost*." *Philological Quarterly* 46 (2): 186–193.

Chen, K. K., and Jensen, H. 1929. "A Pharmacognostic Study of Ch'an Su, the Dried Venom of the Chinese Toad." *Journal of the American Pharmaceutical Association* 18 (3): 244–251.

Chenery, Janet. 1967. *The Toad Hunt*. New York: Harper and Row.

Christiansen, R. T. 1977. *The Migratory Legends*. New York: Arno Press.

Christie, A. 1968. *Chinese Mythology*. London: Paul Hamlyn.

Churcher, S. 1977. "Where Men Are Men, Women Are Women, and Who Cares about Toads?" *Macleans* 90: 52.

Cirlot, J. E. 1962. *A Dictionary of Symbols*. Translated by Jack Sage. London: Routledge and Kegan Paul.

Clarkson, A., and Cross, G. B. 1980. *World Folktales: A Scribner Resource Collection*. New York: Charles Scribner's Sons.

Cochran, D. M. 1961. *Living Amphibians of the World*. Garden City, N.Y: Doubleday.

Coe, M. D., 1965. *The Jaguar's Children: Pre-Classic Central Mexico*. New York: Museum of Primitive Art.

———. 1968. *America's First Civilization*. New York: American Heritage.

———.1978. *Lords of the Underworld: Masterpieces of Classic Maya Ceramics*. Princeton, N. J.: The Art Museum, Princeton University.

Coe, M. D., and Diehl, R. A. 1980. *In the Land of the Olmec*. 2 vols. Austin: University of Texas Press.

Cohn, N. 1975. *Europe's Inner Demons: An Enquiry Inspired by the Great Witch-Hunt*. New York: Basic Books.

Colby, C. T. 1980. "Warty Toads." *Blair & Ketchum's Country Journal* 7 (July): 60–65.

Columbia University Department of Art History and Archaeology. 1968. *Early Chinese Art and the Pacific Basin: A Photographic Exhibition*. New York: Intercultural Arts Press.

Conant, R. 1975. *A Field Guide to Reptiles and Amphibians of Eastern and Central North America*. 2nd ed. Boston: Houghton Mifflin.

Cook, F. R. 1983. *An Analysis of Toads of the* Bufo americanus *Group in a Contact Zone in Central Northern North America*. Ottawa: National Museums of Canada.

Cooper, J. C. 1978. *An Illustrated Encyclopaedia of Traditional Symbols*. London: Thames and Hudson.

Corbière, Tristan. 1873. "Le Crapaud," from *Les Amours Jaunes*, translated as "The Toad" by Vernon Watkins, in *A Mirror for French Poetry: 1840–1940*, ed. Cecily Mackworth. London: George Routledge and Sons.

Cornejo, D. 1982. "Night of the Spadefoot Toad." *Science 82* 3: 62–66.

Cox, G. W. 1984. "Mounds of Mystery." *Natural History* 93 (6): 36–45.

Csath, Geza. 1983. *Opium and Other Stories*. Translated by Jascha Kessler and Charlotte Rogers. New York: Penguin Books.

Culbertson, Nancy. 1976. "Toad in a Flower Pot." *Poet Lore* 71 (2): 48.

Curley, M. J., trans. 1979. *Physiologus*. Austin: University of Texas Press.

Dale-Green, P. 1960. "The Symbolism of the Toad: A Study in Ambivalence." Guild Lecture No. 110, *Guild of Pastoral Psychology*, London.

Daniel, H. 1947. *Hieronymus Bosch*. New York: Hyperion Press.

Danielson, D. 1979. "On Toads and the Justice of God." *Milton Quarterly* 13: 12–14.

Davids, R. C. 1967. "The Mystery of Mima Mounds." *Farm Journal* 91 August: 17.

Davis, S.,and Davis, R. 1974. *Tongues and Totems: Comparative Arts of the Pacific Basin*. Anchorage: Alaska International Art Institute.

Dean, J. 1980. "Encounters between Bombardier Beetles and Two Species of Toads (*Bufo americanus, B. marinus*): Speed of Prey-Capture Does Not Determine Success." *Journal of Comparative Physiology* 135: 41-50.

Defoe, Mark. 1977. "Daughters with Toad." *Carolina Quarterly* 29 (2): 75.

DeGraaf, R. M., and Rudis, D. D. 1983. *Amphibians and Reptiles of New England; Habitats and Natural History*. Amherst: University of Massachusetts Press.

Dickerson, M. C. 1931. *The Frog Book*. Garden City, N. Y.: Doubleday, Doran.

Dickinson, Emily. 1983. *The Complete Poems of Emily Dickinson*. Edited by Thomas H. Johnson. Cambridge: Harvard University Press.

Dioscorides. 1959. *The Greek Herbal of Dioscorides*. Edited by R. T. Gunther. New York: Hafner.

Dole, J. W. 1972. "Homing and Orientation of Displaced Toads, *Bufo americanus*, to Their Home Sites." *Copeia* 1972 (1): 151–158.

Dorfmueller, L. 1974. "Now You See It, Now You Don't." *International Wildlife* 4 (January): 30–31.

Dorson, R. M. 1972. *African Folklore*. Garden City, N. Y.: Doubleday.

Drennan, A. 1983. "What Ever Happened to Bufo the Toad?" *Sky and Telescope* 65 (April): 316–319.

Eberhard, W. 1968. *The Local Cultures of South and East China*. Translated by Alide Eberhard. Leiden: E. J. Brill.

Efron, D. H. ed. 1970. *Psychotomimetic Drugs*. New York: Raven Press.

Egger, F. 1935. *Frosch und Kröte bei den alten Ägyptern*, "Band 4," Mitteilungen der Geographisch-Ethnologischen Gesellschaft, Basel.

Eliade, M. 1964. *Shamanism: Archaic Techniques of Ecstasy*. Translated by W. R. Trask. New York: Bollingen Foundation.

Eliot, George. 1876. *Novels of George Eliot*. Vol. 4. New York: Harper and Brothers.

"Escorting Toads across Highways." 1983. *National Wildlife* 21 (5): 28.

Etter, Dave. 1969. "Firewood Hill." In *31 New American Poets*, ed. R. Schreiber. New York: Hill and Wang.

Ewert, J. P. 1970. "Neural Mechanisms of Prey-Catching and Avoidance Behavior in the Toad (*Bufo bufo* L.)." *Brain, Behavior, and Evolution* 3: 36–56.

Ewert, J. P., and Ingle, D. 1971. "Excitatory Effects Following Habituation of Prey-Catching Activity in Frogs and Toads." *Journal of Comparative and Physiological Psychology* 77: 369–374.

"Extra, Extra! Fly Eats Toad." 1984. *Science 84*, 5 (1): 10, 12.

Fairchild, L. 1981. "Mate Selection and Behavioral Thermoregulation in Fowler's Toads." *Science* 212: 950–951.

Fairchild, L.; Christian, K. A.; and Tracy, C. R. 1983. "Thermoregulation and Mate-Selection in Fowler's Toads?" *Science* 219: 518–519.

Fawcett, Edgar. 1901. "A Toad." In *Songs of Nature*, ed. John Burroughs. New York: McClure Phillips.

Fellows, A. 1969. "Cane Beetles and Toads." *Victorian Naturalist* 86:165.

Ferguson, G. 1954. *Signs and Symbols in Christian Art*. New York: Oxford University Press.

Finkel, Donald. 1966. "Spring Song." In *A Joyful Noise*. New York: Atheneum. Originally published in *The New Yorker*, 22 May, 1965.

Fisher, M. F. K. 1961. *A Cordiall Water*. Boston: Little, Brown.

Flindt, R., and Hemmer, H. 1972. "Studies on the Responses of *Bufo calamita* and *Bufo viridis* to Species-Specific Mating Calls." *Biologisches Zentralblatt* 91: 597–600.

Fogden, M., and Fogden, P. 1984. "All that Glitters May Be Toads." *Natural History* 93 (5): 46–50.

Fouquette, M. J. 1980. "Effect of Environmental Temperatures on Body Temperature of Aquatic-Calling Anurans." *Journal of Herpetology* 14: 347–352.

Fowlie, W. 1973. *Lautréamont*. New York: Twayne.

Francis, E. T. B. 1961. "The Sources and Nature of Salivary Secretions in Amphibia." *Proceedings of the Zoological Society of London* 186: 453–476.

Frazer, J. F. D. 1967. "Amphibians." In *Larousse Encyclopedia of Animal Life*, pp. 268-282. New York: McGraw-Hill.

Freytag, G. E. 1972. "Amphibians." In *Grzimek's Animal Life Encyclopedia*. Vol. 5, pp. 283-308. New York: Van Nostrand Reinhold.

Friedmann, H. 1980. *A Bestiary for St. Jerome: Animal Symbolism in European Religious Art*. Washington, D. C.: Smithsonian Institution Press.

Furst, P. T. ed. 1972a. *Flesh of the Gods: The Ritual Use of Hallucinogens*. New York: Praeger.

————. 1972b. "Symbolism and Psychopharmacology: The Toad as Earth Mother in Indian America." In *Religión en Mesoamerica, XII Mesa Redonda*, pp. 37–46. Mexico: Sociedad Mexicana de Antropologia.

————. 1974. "Hallucinogens in Precolumbian Art." In *Art and Environment in Native America* (The Museum, Special Publications, No. 7), ed. M. E. King and I. R. Traylor, pp. 55–101. Lubbock: Texas Tech Press.

————. 1976. *Hallucinogens and Culture*. San Francisco: Chandler and Sharp.

————. 1981. "Jaguar Baby or Toad Mother: A New Look at an Old Problem in Olmec Iconography." In *The Olmec and Their Neighbors: Essays in Memory of Matthew W. Stirling*, ed. E. P. Benson, pp. 149-162. Washington, D. C.: Dumbarton Oaks.

Gans, C., and Gorniak, G. C. 1982. "How Does the Toad Flip Its Tongue? Test of Two Hypotheses." *Science* 216: 1335–1337.

Gardner, E. E. 1937. *Folklore from The Schoharie Hills, New York*. Ann Harbor: University of Michigan Press.

Gebhart, L. 1967. "Plague of Toads." *Science News* 92 (8 July) 38–39.

Gerhardt, H. C. 1975. "Sound Pressure Levels and Radiation Patterns of the Vocalizations of Some North American Frogs and Toads." *Journal of Comparative Physiology* 102: 1–12.

Gimlette, J. D. 1971. *Malay Poisons and Charm Cures*. London: Oxford University Press.

Gimlette, J. D., and Thomson, H. W. 1939. *A Dictionary of Malay Medicine*. London: Oxford University Press.

Goin, C. J.; Goin, O. B.; and Zug, G. R. 1978. *Introduction to Herpetology*. 3rd ed. San Francisco: W. H. Freeman.

Goldsmith, Oliver. 1900. *The Works of Oliver Goldsmith*. Edited by P. Cunningham. New York: Harper and Brothers.

Gorman, R. R., and Ferguson, J. H. 1970. *Sun-Compass Orientation in the Western Toad*, Bufo boreas. *Herpetologica* 26: 34–45.

Gossman, A. 1976. "Satan: From Toad to Atlas." *Milton Quarterly* 10: 7–11.

Grafton, C. B. 1983. *Konrad Gesner: Beasts and Animals in Decorative Woodcuts of the Renaissance*. New York: Dover.

Grahame, Kenneth. 1933. *The Wind in the Willows*. New York: Charles Scribner's Sons.

Greding, E. J. 1971. "Comparative Rates of Learning in Frogs (*Ranidae*) and Toads (*Bufonidae*)." *Caribbean Journal of Science* 11: 203–208.

Greenberg, J. 1983. "For Whom the Bell? Toads—Poetic Justice in the Arizona Desert." *Science News* 124 (19): 293.

Gresson, R. A. R., and O'Dubhda, S. "Natterjack Toads *Bufo calamita Laur.* at Castlegregory and Fermoyle, Co. Kerry." *Irish Naturalist's Journal* 17: 9–11.

Grottanelli, V. L. 1967. "Zoomorphic and Plant Representations: Pre-Columbian America. In *McGraw-Hill Encyclopedia of World Art*. Vol. 14. New York: McGraw-Hill.

Grubb, J. C. 1970. "Orientation in Post-Reproductive Mexican Toads, *Bufo valliceps*." *Copeia* 1970 (4): 674–680.

———.1973. "Olfactory Orientation in Breeding Mexican Toads, *Bufo valliceps*." *Copeia* 1973 (3): 490–497.

———.1973b. "Olfactory Orientation in *Bufo woodhousei fowleri, Pseudacris clarki* and *Pseudacris streckeri.*" *Animal Behaviour* 21: 726–732.

———.1973c. "Orientation in Newly Metamorphosed Mexican Toads, *Bufo valliceps*." *Herpetologica* 29: 95–100.

Gubernatis, A. de. 1872. *Zoological Mythology*. Vol. 1. Reprint. New York: Arno Press, 1978.

Halliwell-Phillips, J. O. 1856. "Notes to the Second Act of *As You Like It*." In *Works of Shakespeare*, Vol. 6, pp. 130–134. London: J. E. Adlard.

Hamblin, N. L. 1981. "The Magic Toads of Cozumel." *Mexicon* 3 (1): 10–14.

Hand, W. D., ed. 1976. *American Folk Medicine: A Symposium*. Berkeley and Los Angeles: University of California Press.

Harner, M. J. 1973. "The Role of Hallucinogenic Plants in European Witchcraft." In *Hallucinogens and Shamanism*, ed. M. J. Harner, pp. 127–149. New York: Oxford University Press.

Harter, J., ed. 1979. *Animals: 1419 Copyright-Free Illustrations of Mammals, Birds, Fish, Insects, etc.* New York: Dover.

Hawes, Judy. 1969. *What I Like About Toads*. New York: Thomas Y. Crowell.

Heatwole, H., and Heatwole, A. 1968. "Motivational Aspects of Feeding Behavior in Toads." *Copeia* 1968 (4): 692–698.

Hedges, J. S. 1973. "Toads in the Barn." *Tennessee Folklore Society Bulletin* 39:79.

Hemmer, H., and Jakobs, H. 1974. "Functional Correlates of Differences in Body Proportions and Burrowing Behaviour in the Natterjack (*Bufo calamita Laur.*) and the Green Toad (*Bufo viridis Laur.*)." *Forma et Functio* 7: 1-6.

Henderson, F. G.; Welles, J. S.; and Chen, K. K. 1962. "Parotoid Secretions of Indonesian Toads." *Science* 136: 775–776.

Heusser, H. 1970. "Paarungs- und Befreiungsruf der Erdkröte, *Bufo bufo bufo* (L.)." *Zeitschrift für Tierpsychologie* 27: 894–898.

———.1972. "Frogs and Toads," pp. 357–383; "Lower Anurans," pp. 384–396; "Higher Anurans," pp. 397–454. In *Grzimek's Animal Life Encyclopedia*, Vol. 5. New York: Van Nostrand Reinhold.

Hilberry, Conrad. 1982. "Toads." *Kenyon Review* 4 (2): 91–92.

Hodge, R. P. 1976. *Amphibians and Reptiles in Alaska, The Yukon and Northwest Territories*. Anchorage: Alaska Northwest Publishing Co.

Holbrook, J. E. 1976. *North American Herpetology*. Society for the Study of Amphibians and Reptiles. Reprint. Philadelphia: J. Dobson. 1836–40.

Holmes, S. J. 1928. *The Biology of the Frog*. 4th ed. New York: Macmillan.

Hugo, Victor. 1906. "Le Crapaud," from *La Legende des Siècles*. In *Oeuvres Complètes de Victor Hugo*. Vol. 6. Paris: L'Imprimerie Nationale.

Hunt, R. H. 1980. "Toad Sanctuary in a Tarantula Burrow." *Natural History* 89 (3): 48–53.

Hyatt, H. M. 1935. *Folk-Lore from Adams Country, Illinois*. New York: Alma Egan Hyatt Foundation.

Jekyll, W., ed. 1966. "Toad and Donkey." In *Jamaican Song and Story*. New York: Dover.

Jobes, G. 1961. *Dictionary of Mythology, Folklore, and Symbols*. New York: Scarecrow Press.

Jones, A. W. 1979. "Christian Formation and the Moral Quest (from Tadpoles to Toads; from Adam to Christ)." *Anglican Theological Review* 61: 63–86.

Joode, T. de; Stolk, A., and Kiefte, K. de. 1983. "The Toad: Sketches from Nature." *Blair and Ketchum's Country Journal* 10 (May): 34-35.

Joya, M. 1964. *Mock Joya's Things Japanese.* 5th ed., rev. Tokyo: Tokyo News Service.

Kaess, W., and Kaess, F. 1960. "Perception of Apparent Motion in the Common Toad." *Science* 132: 953.

Kelley, D. H. 1976. *Deciphering the Maya Script.* Austin: University of Texas Press.

Kellner, R. S. 1975. "Sex, Toads, and Scorpions: A Study of the Psychological Themes in Melville's *Pierre.*" *Arizona Quarterly* 35: 5–20.

Kennedy, A. B. 1982. "*Ecce Bufo:* The Toad in Nature and in Olmec Iconography." *Current Anthropology* 23 (3): 273–290.

Kennedy, X. J. 1979. "A Visit to the Gingerbread House." In *The Phantom Ice Cream Man.* New York: Atheneum.

Keswick, J. 1977. "Liu Hai and the Three-Legged Toad." *Country Life* 161: 740, 743.

Khmelevskays, N. V. 1972. "On the Role of the Sense of Smell in the Life of Anura." *Zoologicheskii Zhurnal* 51: 764–767.

Kingston, M. H. 1977. *The Woman Warriors.* New York: Vintage Books.

Kipling, Rudyard. 1900. *The Works of Rudyard Kipling.* Boston: Jefferson Press.

Kirkland, A. H. 1904. "Usefulness of the American Toad." Reprinted in *Farmer's Bulletin No. 196*, U.S. Department of Agriculture March 1915.

Kittredge, G. L. 1929. *Witchcraft in Old and New England.* Cambridge, Mass.: Harvard University Press.

Klingender, F. 1971. *Animals in Art and Thought to the End of the Middle Ages.* Cambridge, Mass.: M.I.T. Press.

Koestler, Arthur. 1973. *The Case of the Midwife Toad.* New York: Random House.

Kors, A. C., and Peters, E., eds. 1972. *Witchcraft in Europe, 1100-1700: A Documentary History.* Philadelphia: University of Pennsylvania Press.

Kozloff, A. P., ed. 1981. *Animals in Ancient Art from the Leo Mildenberg Collection.* Bloomington: Indiana University Press.

Krutch, Joseph Wood. 1952. *The Desert Year.* New York: William Sloane Associates.

Kuhn, O., and Thenius, E. 1972. "Origin of the Tetrapods." In *Grzimek's Animal Life Encyclopedia.* Vol. 5, pp. 273–282. New York: Van Nostrand Reinhold.

Kuznets, L. R. 1978. "Toad Hall Revisited." *Children's Literature* 7: 115–128.

Laming, P. R., and Austin, M. 1981. "Cardiac Responses of the Anurans, *Bufo bufo* and *Rana pipiens,* During Behavioural Arousal and Fright." *Comparative Biochemistry and Physiology; A: Comparative Physiology* 68 (3): 515–518.

Lang, Andrew, ed. 1948. *The Blue Fairy Book.* New York: Longmans, Green.

Larkin, Philip. 1955. "Toads." In *The Less Deceived.* Hessle, East Yorkshire (England): Marvell Press.

——— . 1964. "Toads Revisited." In *The Whitsun Weddings.* London: Faber and Faber,

Lautréamont, Comte de. 1972. *Les Chants de Maldoror.* Translated by Alexis Lykiard. New York: Thomas Y. Crowell.

Leeser, O. 1959. "*Bufo.*" *The British Homoeopathic Journal* 48 (3): 176–188.

Lewinsohn, R., trans. 1954. *Animals, Men and Myths.* New York: Harper and Brothers.

Licht, L. E. 1967. "Death Following Possible Ingestion of Toad Eggs." *Toxicon* 5: 141–142.

——— . 1968. "Unpalatability and Toxicity of Toad Eggs." *Herpetologica* 24 (2): 93–98.

Liddell, H. G., and Scott, R. 1940. *A Greek-English Lexicon,* Oxford: Clarendon Press.

Lobel, Arnold. 1970. *Frog and Toad Are Friends.* New York: Harper and Row.

——— . 1972. *Frog and Toad Together.* New York: Harper and Row.

——— . 1976. *Frog and Toad All Year.* New York: Harper and Row.

Loehr, M. 1968. *Ritual Vessels of Bronze Age China.* New York: The Asia Society.

Loewe, M. 1979. *Ways to Paradise: The Chinese Quest for Immortality.* London: Allen and Unwin.

Long, D. E. 1946. "A Toad in Town." *Carnegie Magazine* 19: 212–214.

Lorcher, K. 1969. "Comparative Bio-Acoustic Investigations in the Fire-Bellied Toad and the Yellow-Bellied Toad, *Bombina bombina* (L.) and *Bombina v. variegata* (L.)" *Oecologia* 3:84–124.

Lourdeaux, S. 1982. "Toads in Gardens for Marianne Moore and William Carlos Williams." *Modern Philology* 80 (2): 166–167.

"Love Among the Toads." 1981. *Newsweek,* 8 June, 86.

Love, M. 1981. "With a Little Help from My Friends." *Natural History* 90 (11): 16–19.

Luderer, Lynn Marie. 1982. *The Toad Intruder*. New York: Houghton Mifflin.

Lurker, M. 1980. *The Gods and Symbols of Ancient Egypt: An Illustrated Dictionary*. London: Thames and Hudson.

Luther, Martin. 1902. *The Table Talk of Martin Luther*. Edited by W. Hazlitt. London: George Bell and Sons.

Lyman, L. C., ed. 1957. *Beautyway: A Navaho Ceremonial*. New York: Bollingen Foundation.

Macartney, J. M., and Gregory, P. 1981. "Differential Susceptibility of Sympatric Garter Snake Species to Amphibian Skin Secretions." *American Midland Naturalist* 106 (2): 271–281.

Mackworth, Cecily, ed. 1947. *A Mirror for French Poetry: 1840–1940*. London: George Routledge and Sons.

Mann, Felix. 1959. "The Homoeopathic Toad." *The British Homoeopathic Journal* 48 (3): 189–191.

Marchisin, A., and Anderson, J. D. 1978. "Strategies Employed by Frogs and Toads (Amphibia, anura) to Avoid Predation by Snakes (Reptilia, serpentes)." *Journal of Herpetology* 12 (2): 151–155.

Marquis, Don. 1950. *The Lives and Times of Archy and Mehitabel*. Garden City, N.Y.: Doubleday.

Martin, Charles. 1973. "Orgy With Toads: Erogenous Zones." *Poetry* 123 (3): 156–157.

Martin, W. F. 1971. "Mechanics of Sound Reproduction in Toads of the Genus *Bufo*: Passive Elements." *Journal of Experimental Zoology* 176: 273-294.

Martof, B. 1962. "Some Observations on the Feeding of Fowler's Toad." *Copeia* 1962 (2):439.

McCord, Howard. 1980. *The Great Toad Hunt and Other Expeditions*. Trumansburg, N.Y.: Crossing Press.

McCulloch, F. 1962. *Mediaeval Latin and French Bestiaries*. Chapel Hill: University of North Carolina Press.

McDonald, G. D., ed. 1959. *A Way of Knowing*. New York: Thomas Y. Crowell.

Meyers, R. R. 1972. "Was there a Toad in the Bower?" *Modern Language Quarterly* 33: 37–43.

Michalowski, K. 1969. *Art of Ancient Egypt*. Translated by. N. Guterman. New York: Harry N. Abrams.

Michell, J. 1977. *Phenomena: A Book of Wonders*. New York: Pantheon.

Miller, Carl. 1980. "A Toad Sketched in Ballpoint." *Ball State University Forum* 21 (1): 13.

Milne, A. A. 1929. *Toad of Toad Hall: A Play from Kenneth Grahame's Book*. New York: Charles Scribner's Sons.

Milton, John. 1888. *Paradise Lost*. Edited by. H. C. Walsh. Philadelphia: Henry Altemus.

Montgomery, G. 1977. "Mad Toads and Englishmen." *TV Guide*, 17 Sept., 69-70.

Moore, J. A , ed. 1964. *Physiology of the Amphibia*. New York: Academic Press.

Morris, Desmond. 1980. *Animal Days*. New York: William Morrow.

Moscrip, R. J. 1966. "Water the Hibernating Toads." *NEA Journal* 55 (February): 30–32.

Muñoz, J. 1978. "An Annual Spring Event." *Alaska* 44: 16.

Murray, M. A. 1921. *The Witch-Cult in Western Europe*. Oxford: Clarendon Press.

Myers, P. H. 1857. *The Prisoner of the Border*. New York: Derby and Jackson.

Nadkarni, K. M. 1955. *Indian Materia Medica*. Revised by A. K. Nadkarni. Vol. 2. Bombay: Popular Press.

Neill, W. E., and Grubb, J. C. 1971. "Arboreal Habits of *Bufo valliceps* in Central Texas." *Copeia* 1971 (2): 347–348.

The New Yorker Book of Poems. 1969. New York: Viking Press.

Nickolson, H. B. 1983. *Art of Aztec Mexico: Treasures of Tenochtitlan*. Washington D. C.: National Gallery of Art.

"Now You See It . . . Now You Don't!" 1974. *International Wildlife* 4 (January): 30–31.

Oldham, R. S. 1966. "Spring Movements in the American Toad, *Bufo americanus*." *Canadian Journal of Zoology* 44: 63–100.

Oliver, J. A. 1955. *The Natural History of North American Amphibians and Reptiles*. Princeton, N. J.: Van Nostrand.

Opie, I., and Opie, P. 1974. *The Classic Fairy Tales*. London: Oxford University Press.

Ortega, P. D. 1970. "The Toad and the Spider: Paradox and Irony in Browning's Poetry." *The Baratreview* 5: 75–81.

Orwell, George. 1946. "Some Thoughts on the Common Toad." In *Shooting an Elephant and Other Essays*. New York: Harcourt, Brace and World.

Overmann, S. R. 1970. "Social Facilitation of Feeding in Box Turtles and American Toads." *American Zoologist* 10: 473.

Pace, A. 1971. "Sage and Toad: A Boccaccian Motif." *Italica* 48: 187–199.

Palmer, K. 1976. *The Folklore of Somerset.* Totowa, N. J.: Rowman and Littlefield.

Parrinder, Geoffrey. 1971. *A Dictionary of Non-Christian Religions.* Philadelphia: Westminster Press.

Parsons, L. A. 1980. *Pre-Columbian Art.* New York: Harper and Row.

Parsons, T. S. 1967. "Evolution of the Nasal Structure in the Lower Tetrapods." *American Zoologist* 7: 397–413.

Perenyi, E. 1981. *Green Thoughts: A Writer in the Garden.* New York: Random House.

Pistorius, A. 1984. "Focus on Frogs." *U.S. Air* 6 (6): 38–46.

Pliny. 1963. *Natural History.* Translated by W. H. S. Jones. Cambridge, Mass.: Harvard University Press.

Pope, R. 1979. "A Sly Toad, Physiognomy and the Problem of Deceit: Henryson's *The Paddok and the Mous.*" *Neophilologus* 63: 461–468.

Porter, G. 1967. *The World of the Frog and the Toad.* New York: J. B. Lippincott.

Porter, K. R. 1972. *Herpetology.* Philadelphia: W. B. Saunders.

Potter, R. K. 1962. "From Deepest to the Highest." *Audubon Magazine* 64: 147.

Praz, M. 1964. *Studies in Seventeenth-Century Imagery.* 2nd ed. Rome: Edizioni di Storia e Letteratura.

Putnam, R. W., and Hillman, S. S. 1977. "Activity Responses of Anurans to Dehydration." *Copeia* 1977 (4): 746–749.

Rabb, G. 1961. "The Surinam Toad." *Natural History* 70 (May): 40–45.

Radford, E., and Radford, M. A. 1969. *Encyclopaedia of Superstitions.* Westport, Conn.: Greenwood Press.

Raisor, Philip. 1982. "Toads Breeding, Thumb Swelling." *Poetry* 23 (4): 18–19.

Randolph, V. 1947. *Ozark Superstitions.* New York: Columbia University Press.

Read, B. E. 1982. *Chinese Materia Medica.* Reprint. Peking Natural History Bulletin, 1931. Taipei: Southern Materials Center.

Reichard, G. A. 1950. *Navaho Religion: A Study of Symbolism.* Vol. 2. New York: Bollingen Foundation.

Reichel-Dolmatoff, G. 1971. *Amazonian Cosmos: The Sexual and Religious Symbolism of the Tukano Indians.* Chicago: University of Chicago Press.

Reichel-Dolmatoff, G., and Reichel-Dolmatoff, A. 1961. *The People of Aritama: The Cultural Personality of a Colombian Mestizo Village.* Chicago: University of Chicago Press.

Renard, Jules. 1899. *Histoires Naturelles.* Paris: H. Floury.

Richter, G. M. A. 1930. *Animals in Greek Sculpture.* New York: Oxford University Press.

Ricks, Christopher. 1981. "The Pink Toads in *Lord Jim.*" *Essays in Criticism* 31 (2): 142–144.

Riley, J. W. 1913. *The Works of James Whitcomb Riley.* New York: Charles Scribner's Sons.

Risser, J. 1914. "Olfactory Reactions in Amphibians." *Journal of Experimental Zoology* 16: 617–652.

Robbins, R. H. 1959. *The Encyclopedia of Witchcraft and Demonology.* New York: Crown Publishers.

Robin, P. A. 1970. *Animal Lore in English Literature.* London: Folcroft Press.

Rockcastle, V. N. 1961. "Amphibians." *Cornell Science Leaflet* 54 (4): 3–32.

Roskoff, G. 1869. *Geschichte des Teufels.* Leipzig. Reprint. Aalen: Scientia Verlag, 1967.

Rossetti, Dante Gabriel. 1886. "Jenny." In *The Collected Works of Dante Gabriel Rossetti*, Vol. 1. London: Ellis and Scrutton.

Roth, W. E. 1915. "An Inquiry into the Animism and Folk-Lore of the Guiana Indians." Thirtieth Annual Report of the Bureau of American Ethnology. Washington, D. C.: Government Printing Office.

Rowlands, J. 1979. *The Garden of Earthly Delights: Hieronymus Bosch.* Oxford: Phaidon Press.

Rugh, R. 1951. *The Frog: Its Reproduction and Development.* New York: McGraw-Hill.

Runes, D. D., and Schrickel, H. G., eds. 1946. *Encyclopedia of the Arts.* New York: Philosophical Library.

Russell, J. B. 1972. *Witchcraft in the Middle Ages.* Ithaca, N. Y.: Cornell University Press.

Salmon, W. 1691. *The New London Dispensatory.* London: T. Bassett.

San Francisco Examiner, 7 March, 1984.

Santora, P. 1984. "Of Kings and Spadefoots." *The Conservationist* 38: 46–49.

Schaeffer, Susan Fromberg. 1975. *The Rhymes and Runes of the Toad.* New York: Macmillan.

Schmajuk, N., and Segura, E. T. 1971. "Modelo del Comportamiento Sexual de los Anuros." *Sociedad Argentina de Biologia Revista* 47: 40–56.

Schoenknecht, C. A. 1960. *Frogs and Toads.* Chicago: Follett.

Schreiber, R., 1969. *31 New American Poets.* New York: Hill and Wang

Schultes, R. E., and Hofmann, A. 1980. *The Botany and Chemistry of Hallucinogens.* Rev. ed. Springfield, Ill.: Charles C. Thomas.

Scott, Sir Walter. 1900. *Rob Roy*. New York: Harper and Brothers.

Shakespeare, William. 1856. *Works of Shakespeare*. Edited by J. O. Halliwell-Phillips. London: J. E. Adlard.

Sheldon, Lyons, and Roualt, eds. 1965. *The Reading of Poetry*. Newton, Mass.: Allyn & Bacon.

Shepard, L. 1978. *The Broadside Ballad: A Study in Origins and Meaning*. Hatboro, Penn.: Legacy Books.

Sherman, C. K., and Morton, M. L. 1984. "The Toad that Stays on Its Toes." *Natural History* 93: 72–78.

Shinn, E. A., and Dole, J. W. 1979. "Evidence for a Role for Olfactory Cues in the Feeding Response of Western Toads, *Bufo boreas*." *Copeia* 1979 (1): 163–165.

————. 1979b. "Lipid Components of Prey Odors Elicit Feeding Responses in Western Toads (*Bufo boreas*)." *Copeia* 1979 (2): 275–278.

Shortt, T. M. 1982. "My Love Affair with Toads." *International Wildlife* 12 (January–February): 25–29.

Skelton, Robin. 1969. "Toad." *Poetry* 115 (3): 162–163.

Smiley, T. 1982. "A Boyhood Spring that Couldn't be Whipped Got Hopping with 28 Toads." *Sports Illustrated*, 8 Nov., 102, 104.

Smith, H. M. 1978. *Amphibians of North America: A Guide to Field Identification*. New York: Golden Press.

Snelling, J. C. 1969. "A Raptor Study in the Kruger National Park." *Bokmakierie* 21 (suppl. 3): 7–10.

Spencer, K. 1957. *An Analysis of Navaho Chantway Myths*. Philadelphia: American Folklore Society.

Spenser, Edmund. Edited by J. C. Smith. 1909. *The Poetical Works of Edmund Spenser*. Oxford, Clarendon Press.

Stafford, William. 1983. *Smoke's Way*. Port Townsend, Wash.: Graywolf Press.

Steel, R., ed. 1979. *Encyclopedia of Prehistoric Life*. New York: McGraw-Hill.

Stern, J., ed. 1944. *The Complete Grimm's Fairy Tales*. New York: Random House.

Steward, O. M. 1971. "Fowler's Toad Attacked by Eastern Chipmunk." *Engelhardtia* 4 (2): 14.

Stoker, B. 1965. *Dracula*. New York: New American Library.

Szentleleky, T. 1969. *Ancient Lamps*. Budapest: Akademiai Kiado.

Tandy, M., et al. 1976. "A New Species of *Bufo* (Anura: Bufonidae) from Africa's Dry Savannas." *Pearce Sellards Series; Texas Memorial Museum*, No. 24: 1–20.

Taylor, Jane. 1925. "The Toad's Journal." In *The Library of Poetry and Song*, Vol. 3, ed. William Cullen Bryant. New York: Doubleday, Page.

Thomas, K. 1971. *Religion and the Decline of Magic*. London: Weidenfeld and Nicolson.

————. 1983. *Man and the Natural World: A History of the Modern Sensibility*. New York: Pantheon Books.

Thompson, J., trans. 1877. *Public and Private Life of Animals*. Illustrated by J. J. Grandville. London: Sampson Low, Marston, Searle, and Rivington.

Thompson, J. E. S. 1970. *Maya History and Religion*. Norman: University of Oklahoma Press.

Thompson, W. T. 1845. *Chronicles of Pineville*. Philadelphia: Carey and Hart.

Thorndike, L. 1923. *A History of Magic and Experimental Science* . Vols. 1–2. New York: Macmillan.

————. 1934–1958. *A History of Magic and Experimental Science*. Vols. 3–8. New York: Columbia University Press.

"A Toad Serves the Sugar Industry of Puerto Rico." 1949. *Research Achievement Sheet 118 (0)*. Washington, D. C.: U.S. Department of Agriculture, Agricultural Research Administration.

Toft, C. A. 1980. "Feeding Ecology of Thirteen Syntopic Species of Anurans in a Seasonal Tropical Environment." *Oecologia* 45: 131–141.

Topsell, E. 1658. *The History of Four-Footed Beasts*, I. Reprint 1967. New York: Da Capo Press.

Toulouse-Lautrec, Henri de. 1896. Illustration for "Les Deux Soeurs Lègendaires." *Le Figaro Illustré* 74 (May): 88.

Toynbee, J. M. C. 1973. *Animals in Roman Life and Art*. Ithaca, N. Y.: Cornell University Press.

Tracy, C. R., 1971. "Evidence for the Use of Celestial Cues by Dispersing Immature California Toads (Bufo boreas)." Copeia 1971 (1): 145–147.

Tracy, C. R. and Dole, J. W. 1969. "Orientation of Displaced California Toads, *Bufo boreas*, to Their Breeding Sites." *Copeia* 1969 (4): 693–700.

Treat, D. A. 1948. *Frogs and Toads*. New York: National Audubon Society.

Twain, Mark. 1955. *Pudd'nhead Wilson*. New York: Grove Press.

"Undogmatic Toad." 1980. *Scientific American* 242: 66, 68, 69.

Untermeyer, Louis, ed. 1935. *Rainbow in the Sky*. New York: Harcourt, Brace.

Virgil. *Eclogues and Georgics*. Translated by T. F. Royds. 1946. London: J. M. Dent and Sons.

Volker, T. 1950. *The Animal in Far Eastern Art*. Leiden: E. J. Brill.

Wagoner, David. 1969. "A Valedictory to Standard Oil of Indiana." In *The New Yorker Book of Poems* (1969). New York: Viking Press.

Wainio, A. 1970. "Nature—the Master Pest Exterminator." *Ontario Fish and Wildlife Review* 9 (3–4): 16–22.

Walkowiak, W. 1980. "The Coding of Auditory Signals in the Torus Semicircularis of the Firebellied Toad and the Grass Frog: Responses to Simple Stimuli and to Conspecific Calls." *Journal of Comparative Physiology* 138: 131–148.

Walkowiak, W.; Capranica, R. R.; and Schneider, H. 1981. "A Comparative Study of Auditory Sensitivity in the Genus *Bufo* (Amphibia)." *Behavioural Processes* 6: 223–237.

Wallace, D. R. 1981. "Gardening with Pests." *Blair & Ketchum's Country Journal* 8 (Aug.): 66–71.

Wallace, Robert. 1968. "Ungainly Things." New York: E. P. Dutton.

Wallis, C. 1983. "Zombies: Do They Exist?" *Time* 122 (17): 60.

Warner, C. D. 1885. *My Summer in a Garden*. Boston: Houghton, Mifflin.

Wassen, H. 1934. "The Frog in Indian Mythology and Imaginative World." *Anthropos* 29: 613–658.

Wasserman, A. O. 1966. "It Could Be a Froad; Maybe a Trog." *Natural History* 75 (April): 18–23.

Wassersug, R. 1984. "Why Tadpoles Love Fast Food." *Natural History* 93 (4): 60–68.

Wasson, R. G. 1968. *Soma: Divine Mushroom of Immortality*. New York: Harcourt, Brace and World.

Watt, Ian. 1979. *Conrad in the Nineteenth Century*. Berkeley and Los Angeles: University of California Press.

Wauchope, R. H., ed. 1965. *Handbook of Middle American Indians*. Austin: University of Texas Press.

Weber, E. 1976. "Alterations in the Release Calls of Six European Anura (Amphibia) after Partial or Total Extirpation of the Vocal Cords." *Behavioural Processes* 1: 197–216.

White, B. 1954. "Medieval Animal Lore." *Anglia: Zeitschrift für Englische Philologie* 72: 21–30.

White, C. J. 1984. "Friend Charlie, the Toad." *Gardens For All News* 7 (4): 27.

Wickler, W., and Seibt, U. 1974. "Rufen und Antworten bei *Kassina senegalensis, Bufo regularis* und anderen Anuren." *Zeitschrift für Tierpsychologie* 34: 524–537.

——— 1982. "Toad Spawn Symbolism Suggested for Sechin." *American Antiquity* 47 (2):441–444.

Wilbur, H. M.; Rubenstein, D. I.; and Fairchild, L. 1978. "Sexual Selection in Toads: The Roles of Female Choice and Male Body Size." Evolution 32 (2): 264–270.

Wilbur, Richard. 1950. "The Death of a Toad." In *Ceremony and Other Poems*. London: Faber and Faber.

Williams. C. A. S. 1960. *Encyclopedia of Chinese Symbolism and Art Motives*. New York: Julian Press.

Williams, Paul O. 1978. "Shoveling a Toad." *Poet Lore* 73 (1): 7.

Williams, William Carlos. 1951. "Romance Moderne." In *The Collected Earlier Poems of William Carlos Williams*. New York: New Directions.

Wilson, Nancy. 1974. "Ode to a Toad." *Saturday Evening Post* 246 (October): 56–57.

Wootton, A. C. 1910. *Chronicles of Pharmacy*. Vol. 1. Reprint. Boston: Milford House, 1971.

Wright, A. H. 1914. *North American Anura*. Washington, D.C: Carnegie Institution.

Wright, A. H., and Wright, A. A. 1949. *Handbook of Frogs and Toads of the United States and Canada*. Ithaca, N.Y.: Comstock Publishing.

Wright, R. H. 1969. "The Disappearing Toad." *Science Digest* 65: 29–31.

Yaremko, R. M.; Jette, J.; and Utter, W. 1974. "Further Study of Avoidance Conditioning in Toads." *Bulletin of the Psychonomic Society* 3: 340–342.

Yeats, William Butler. 1989. *The Poems of W. B. Yeats: A New Edition,* ed. R. J. Finneran. New York: Macmillan.

Zim, H. S. 1950. *Frogs and Toads*. New York: William Morrow.

Zingg, R. M. 1938. *The Huichols: Primitive Artists*. New York: G. E. Stechert. Reprint. Millwood, N.Y.: Kraus Reprint, 1977.

Zug, G. R., and Zug, P. B. 1979. *The Marine Toad*, Bufo marinus: *A Natural History Resume of Native Populations*. Washington, D.C.: Smithsonian Institution Press.

INDEX